GOD loves you

GOD loves you

Charles Spurgeon

Whitaker House

All Scripture quotations are from the *King James Version* (KJV) of the Bible.

GOD LOVES YOU

ISBN: 0-88368-499-3
Printed in the United States of America

Whitaker House
30 Hunt Valley Circle
New Kensington, PA 15068

2 3 4 5 6 7 8 9 10 11 12 / 06 05 04 03 02 01 00 99 98 97

Contents

Chapter 1

Life's Need and Maintenance

None can keep alive his own soul.
—Psalm 22:29

We must begin by noticing the first meaning of these words. There is a day coming when the true God will be acknowledged as Lord and God by all mankind, as we see in verse twenty-seven: *"All the ends of the world shall remember and turn unto the LORD: and all the kindreds of the nations shall worship before thee."* In that day, the greatest of men will bow before Him. The verse from which we take our text says, *"All they that be fat upon earth shall eat and worship."* The prosperous ones, those who have grown rich and great, will receive good at the hands of the Savior and will rejoice to adore Him as the Author of their prosperity. Kings will acknowledge Him as their King, and lords will accept Him as their Lord. Then, not only the riches of life, but also the poverty of death, will render Him homage. As men will go down to the dust of the grave, in their feebleness and weakness they will look up to Him for strength and solace, and they will find it sweet to worship Him in death. Men will know that the keys of death are in His hands (Rev. 1:18).

"All they that go down to the dust shall bow before him" (Ps. 22:29), and it will be known all the world over that the events and purposes of life are in the hands of Jesus Christ. All men will understand that He has been appointed as Mediator to rule over all mortal things, for *"the government shall be upon his shoulder"* (Isa. 9:6). He will open and no man will shut, and He will shut and no man will open (Isa. 22:22), for it is His sovereign prerogative to kill and to make alive (Deut. 32:39), and *"none can keep alive his own soul."*

I hold the expectant belief that this dispensation will not come to an end, as some people believe, until the world has been won for Christ. Surely, *"all kings shall fall down before him: all nations shall serve him"* (Ps. 72:11). The shame of the Cross will be followed by honor and glory, for *"men shall be blessed in him: all nations shall call him blessed"* (v. 17). I am more convinced every day, the more I read the Scriptures, that the disheartening views of some interpreters are not true; and I firmly believe that before the whole of prophecy is worked out into history, *"the kingdoms of this world* [will] *become the kingdoms of our Lord, and of his Christ"* (Rev. 11:15).

But there is a more spiritual meaning to consider, which I believe to be as truly the sense of the passage as the first meaning. If you read the psalm carefully, you will notice, when you come to the end of it, that our Savior seems to delight Himself in being made food for the saved ones among the sons of men. In the twenty-sixth verse He says, *"The meek shall eat and be satisfied."* Here He is thinking of the poor among men, to whom He has always been the source of abounding comfort. To them His Gospel has been preached. Thousands of them have found in Him food for their souls that has satisfied them, filled their mouths with praise, and made their hearts live forever. The poor from *"the highways and hedges"* (Luke 14:23) feast to the full at His royal table. Indeed, the blind and the lame, the very beggars of the streets, are among His household guests.

Christ is very mindful of the poor and needy. He redeems their souls from deceit and violence, and their blood is precious in His sight. (See Psalm 72:12–14.) Especially do the poor in spirit feed on Jesus. Over them He pronounced the first benediction of the Sermon on the Mount, and of them He declares, *"Theirs is the kingdom of heaven"* (Matt. 5:3). What a feast do poor, perishing spirits enjoy in Jesus when His flesh becomes to them meat indeed, and His blood becomes drink indeed (John 6:55).

The act of feeding upon Christ does not end here, for in the twenty-ninth verse of Psalm 22 we read of it again. Not only do the poor feed upon the Bread of Heaven, but the great, the rich, and the strong live upon Him, too. *"All they that be fat upon earth shall eat and worship"* (v. 29). There is no other way of life for them, for *"none can keep alive his own soul."* The saints, too, when they have grown in grace, when they have satisfied their hunger and are fat and flourishing in the courts of the Lord's house, must still eat of the same heavenly food. The fat need Jesus as much as the lean, the strong as much as the feeble, for none can do without Him: *"none can keep alive his own soul."* Thus the rich and the poor meet together, and Jesus is the food for them all. The empty and the full alike draw near to the

Redeemer's fullness and receive *"grace for grace"* (John 1:16).

Among those who feel their need of Jesus, there are some of a mournful type of character, who consider themselves ready to perish. They dare not number themselves among the meek who will eat and be satisfied, much less could they think of themselves as the *"fat upon earth"* who will eat and worship. Instead, they stand back from the feast as if they are utterly unworthy to draw near. They dare not believe themselves to be spiritually alive unto God (Rom. 6:11); they reckon themselves among those that go down into the pit (Ps. 28:1); they bear the sentence of death in themselves (2 Cor. 1:9) and are prisoners under bondage through fear (Heb. 2:15).

Their sense of sin and personal unworthiness is so conspicuous and so painful that they are afraid to claim the privileges of living in Zion. They fear that their faith is expiring, their love is dying out, their hope is withered, and their joy has entirely departed. They compare themselves to a dimly burning wick and think themselves to be even more offensive than the nauseous smell given forth by a smoking wick.

To such comes the word that precedes my text: *"They that go down to the dust shall bow before him"* (Ps. 22:29). Christ will be worshipped even by them; their last moments will be cheered by His presence. Through depression of spirit, through the assaults of Satan, and through inability to see the work of the Spirit in their souls, they will be brought so low as to be down to the dust. They will then be lifted up from their misery and made to rejoice in the Lord their Redeemer, who will say to them, *"Shake thyself from the dust; arise, and sit down...loose thyself from the bands of thy neck, O captive daughter of Zion"* (Isa. 52:2).

When souls are brought down this far, they begin to learn for themselves that *"none can keep alive his own soul."* A poor, brokenhearted spirit knows this, for he fears that the inner life within his soul is at its last gasp, and he is afraid that his faith and love and all his graces will be as bones scattered at the grave's mouth (Ps. 141:7). Then he learns what I hope we will believe without having painful experiences to teach it to us, namely, that none of us can keep his own soul alive. In order to preserve our spirits, we must have food continually from above and visitations from the Lord. We do not find life in ourselves, but in our Lord. Apart from Him we could not exist spiritually, even for a moment. We cannot keep our own souls alive through any grace of our own. With this in mind, we will now consider four important ideas.

Sustained by God

First, the inner life must be sustained by God. We are absolutely dependent upon God for the preservation of our spiritual lives. All of us know that none of us can make his own soul live. *"Thou hast destroyed thyself"* (Hos. 13:9), but you cannot make yourself live again. Spiritual life must always be the gift of God. It must come from without; it cannot arise from within. Between the ribs of death, life never takes its birth; how could it? Can the ocean produce fire, or darkness create light? You can go to the charnel house, that dark chamber where the bodies and bones of the dead have been deposited, as often as you like. However, unless the trumpet of the resurrection sounds there, the dry bones will remain in their corruption. The sinner is *"dead in trespasses and sins"* (Eph. 2:1), and he will never have even so much as a right desire toward God, nor a pulse of spiritual life, until Jesus Christ, who is *"the resurrection, and the life"* (John 11:25), quickens him.

Now, it is important for us to remember that we are as much dependent on the Lord

Jesus and the power of His Spirit for being kept alive as we were for being made alive at the first. *"None can keep alive his own soul."* Do you remember when you first depended on Christ for everything? That same entire dependence must be exercised every day of your life.

If you can remember your former nakedness, your poverty, your emptiness, your misery, your death, apart from Christ, then remember that the case would not be one bit better if you could now be separated from sin. If now you have any grace or any holiness or any love, you derive it entirely from Him, and from moment to moment His grace must be continued toward you. Surely, if the connection between you and Christ should by any possibility be severed, you would cease to live spiritually. That is the truth I want to make clear to you.

Despite how it may seem, this is not at all inconsistent with the undying nature of the spiritual life. When we were born again, there was imparted to us a new and higher nature, which is called the spirit. This is a fruit of the Spirit of God, and it can never die. It is an *"incorruptible* [seed]...*which liveth and abideth for ever"* (1 Pet. 1:23). When it is imparted to the soul, it makes us *"partakers of the divine nature"* (2 Pet. 1:4). It keeps us so that the Evil One cannot touch us (1 John 5:18) in such a way as utterly to destroy us. Yet this fact is quite consistent with the assertion that we cannot keep our own souls alive, for we live only because the Lord keeps us alive. The newborn nature is safe because the Lord protects it; it survives the deadly influences of the world because the Lord continues to quicken it. Our new natures are united to the person of Christ, and we live because He lives. We are not kept alive by independent power but by perpetual renewal from the Lord.

This is true of every man living. *"None can keep alive his own soul"*—no, not one. You young people think, perhaps, that older Christians manage better than you do. You imagine that their experience preserves them, but, indeed, they cannot keep their own souls alive any more than you can. You tried and tempted ones sometimes look with envy upon those who dwell at ease, as though their spirituality was self-supporting. But they cannot keep their own souls alive any more than you can. You know your own difficulties, but you do not know those of others. Rest assured, however, that all men have such difficulties and that no man can keep his own soul alive.

This is the truth at all times: at no one moment can we keep ourselves alive. When you are sitting in God's house of prayer, you may dream that you can keep yourself alive there, but it is not so. You might sin the foulest of sins in your heart while sitting there, and you might grieve the Holy Spirit and cloud your life for years while worshipping among the people of God. You are not able to keep your own soul alive in even your happiest and holiest moments. From your knees you might rise to blaspheme, and from the communion table you might go to the seat of the scorner (Ps. 1:1) if you were left to yourself.

All our strength at once would fail us,
If deserted, Lord, by thee;
Nothing then could aught avail us,
Certain our defeat would be:
Those who hate us
Thenceforth their desire would see.

I seldom find myself so much in danger as when I have been in close communion with God. After the most ecstatic devotion, one is hardly prepared for the coarse temptations of this wicked world. When we, like Moses, come down from the mount, if we encounter open sin, we are likely to grow indignant and break all the commandments in the vehemence of our wrath. The sudden change from the highest and holiest contemplations to the trifles and vexations of earth causes the soul to endure such a severe trial that the poet did well to say,

> We should suspect some danger nigh
> When we perceive too much delight.

Even when our delight is of a spiritual kind, we are likely to be off our guard after having been filled with it, and then Satan avails himself of the opportunity. We are never safe unless the Lord keeps us. If we could take you, my brother or sister, place you in the society of saints, tell you to keep the Sabbath day, make every meal a sacrament, and give you nothing to say or do except what would be directly calculated to promote the glory of God, even there you still could not keep your own soul alive. If Adam in perfection could not keep himself in Paradise, how can his imperfect children be so proud as to rely upon their own steadfastness? If among angels there were those who could not keep their first position, how will man hope to stand unless he is upheld?

Why is this? How do we know that our text is true? We gather arguments from the analogies of nature. We do not find that we can keep our own bodies alive. We need divine preservation, or disease and death will soon make us their prey. Our mortal existence is in no way self-contained; no, not even for five minutes can any one of us live upon himself. Take away the air that we breathe, and who could keep himself alive? The lungs need their portion of air, and if they cannot be satisfied, the man soon becomes a corpse. Deprive us of food, leave us for a week without food or drink, and see if we can keep our natural souls alive. Take away from us the means of warmth in the time when cold weather prevails, and death would soon ensue.

Now, if the physical life cannot be sustained by itself, how much less can the higher and spiritual life sustain itself? It must have food; it must have the Spirit to sustain it. The Scriptures present to us the illustrations of a member of the body that dies if it is severed from the vital organs (see 1 Corinthians 12:14–21), and of the branch that is dried up if it is cut off from the stem. (See John 15:5–6.) Toplady poetically expressed the thought when he wrote,

> Quicken'd by thee, and kept alive,
> I flourish and bear fruit;

My life I from thy sap derive,
My vigour from thy root.

I can do nothing without thee;
My strength is wholly thine:
Wither'd and barren should I be,
If sever'd from the vine.

A certain lamp may burn well, but its ability to shine in the future is dependent upon a fresh supply of oil. The ship in rapid motion borrows force from the continuance of the wind, but the sails hang idle if the gale ceases. The river is full to the bank, but if the clouds were never again to pour out their floods, it would become a dry path. All things depend on other things, and everything depends upon the Great Supreme. Nothing is self-sustained. Except for God Himself, no being necessarily exists. Even immortal souls are only so because He has set His seal upon them and declared that they will inherit eternal life, or in consequence of sin they will sink into everlasting punishment. Hence, we are sure that *"none can keep alive his own soul."*

But we do not need to rely on analogies; we can put the matter to the test. Could any believer among us keep any one of his graces alive? You, perhaps, are a sufferer, and until now you have been enabled to be patient. But suppose that the Lord Jesus were to withdraw His presence from you and your pains were to return again. Where would your patience be then? Or, let us suppose you are a Christian worker and have done great things for the Lord; like Samson, you have been exceptionally strong. But if the Lord were withdrawn even once, if He were to leave you to attempt His work alone, you would soon discover that you are as weak as other men and would utterly fail.

We find another instance of this in the matter of holy joy. Did you rejoice in the Lord this morning when you woke? It is very sweet to wake up and hear the birds singing within your heart, but you cannot maintain that joy, no, not even for an hour, no matter what you do. "*'All my springs are in thee'* (Ps. 87:7), my God, and if I am to joy and rejoice, You must anoint me continually with *'the oil of gladness'* (Ps. 45:7)."

Have you not sometimes thought in the morning, "I feel so peaceful and calm, so resigned to the divine will! I think I will be able to keep up this peaceful spirit all day long"? Perhaps you have done so, and if so, I know you have praised God for it. But if you have become angry or bothered at all during the day, you have learned again that *"to will is present with* [you]; *but how to perform that which is good* [you] *find not"* (Rom. 7:18). Well, if we are dependent upon the Lord for any one fruit of the Spirit, how much more will this be true regarding the essential life from which each of these graces springs?

This truth is equally illustrated by our need for help in every part of the spiritual life. Have you ever tried to perform any spiritual act apart from the divine power? What a dull, dead affair it becomes! What a mechanical thing prayer is without the Spirit of God! It is nothing more than the noise of a parrot, a weariness, the drudgery of a slave. How sweet it is to pray when the Spirit gives us faith, power, boldness, fervency, and expectancy in our pleas! But if the Spirit of God is absent from us in prayer, our infirmities prevail against us, and our supplication loses all prevalence.

Perhaps you have vowed to praise God and have gone into a congregation where the sweetest psalms were being sent to heaven. Were you able to praise God until the Holy Spirit came like a divine wind and loosed the fragrance of the flowers of your soul? Perhaps you used the sacred words of the sweet singers of Israel, but your hosannas became weak, and your devotion died. You could not do it.

I know from experience that it is dreadful work to have to preach when one is not conscious of the aid of the Spirit of God! It is like trying to pour water out of dry buckets or trying to feed hungry souls out of empty baskets. A true sermon, the kind that God will bless, no man can preach of himself; he might as well try to sound the archangel's trumpet. We must have You, O blessed Spirit, or we fail! O God, we must have Your power, or every action that we perform is but the movement of a robot and not the acceptable act of a living, spiritual man.

Have you not been regularly reminded by your own blunderings and failings that you cannot keep alive your own soul, especially when you have resolved to be very wise and correct? Have you ever gotten into a self-sufficient mindset and said, "Now, I will never fall into that temptation again, for I am the burnt child who fears the fire," and yet you have fallen again into that very sin? Have you not said, "Well, I understand it all perfectly well. There is no need to wait upon God for direction in so simple a matter, for I am quite experienced in every detail relating to it, and I can manage the affair very well"? And have you not acted as foolishly in the whole matter as the Israelites did in the affair of the Gibeonites, when they were deceived by the old, patched shoes and the moldy bread, and asked no counsel of the Lord? (See Joshua 9:1–14.)

Our strength, whenever we have any, is our greatest weakness, and our imagined wisdom is our real folly. When we are weak, then we are strong (2 Cor. 12:10). When we have a sense of entire dependence upon God and dare not trust ourselves, then we are both wise and safe. Go, young man, even you who are a zealous Christian, go into the house of business without your morning prayer, and see what will befall you. Venture, my sister, to care for your little family without having called upon God for guidance, and see what you will do. Go with a strong resolve that you will never be guilty of the weakness that dishonored you a few days ago, and depend upon the strength of your own will and the firmness of your own purpose, and see if you do not discover before long, to your shame, how great your weakness is. Then again, do not try even one of these experiments, but listen to the word that tells you *"none can keep alive his own soul."*

And now, if anyone should think that he can keep his own soul alive, let me ask him to look at the enemies that surround him. A sheep in the midst of wolves is safe compared with the Christian in the midst of ungodly men. The world waylays us, the Devil assaults us, and behind every bush there lurks a foe. A spark in mid-ocean is not more besieged, a worm is not more defenseless. If the sight of foes around us is not enough to make us confess our danger, let us look at the foes within.

There is enough within your soul, O Christian, though you are one of the best of saints, to destroy you in an hour unless the grace of God guards you and keeps your passions in check and prevents your stubborn will from asserting its own rebellious determinations. Oh, how ready to burst into the flame of sin is the human heart, even at its best. If some of us have not been blown up, it has been more because Providence has kept away the sparks than because of any lack of explosives within. Oh, may God keep us, for if He leaves us, we will not need any Devil to destroy us, but we will prove to be devils to ourselves. We will need no tempters except the oppressing lust for evil that now conceals itself so craftily within our own beings.

We may be quite sure that *"none can keep alive his own soul"* when we remember that provision is made in the Gospel for keeping our souls alive. The Holy Spirit is given so that He may continually quicken and preserve us, and Jesus Christ Himself lives so that we may live also. What purpose would all the splendid provisions and the special safeguards of the covenant of grace have for the preservation of the spiritual life, if that spiritual life could preserve itself? Why does the Lord declare, *"I the LORD do keep it"* (Isa. 27:3), if it can keep itself? The granaries of Egypt, so full of corn, remind us that there is a famine in the land of Canaan; likewise, the treasures laid up in Christ Jesus assure us that we are in need of them. God's supplies are never superfluous, but are meant to meet real needs. Let us, then, all acknowledge that no man among us can keep alive his own soul.

All for His Glory

This brings me, secondly, to notice that this truth brings glory to Christ. Weak-minded professors of faith are prone to trust in men, but they have here an evident warning against such folly. How can they trust in men, who cannot keep their own souls alive? How could I crouch at the feet of another man and ask him to hear my confession and absolve me, when I know that he cannot keep his own soul alive? How could I look up to him and call him "father in God" and expect to receive grace from the laying on of his hands, when I have learned that he is a weak, sinful being like myself? If he cannot keep his own soul alive, what can he do for me? If he lives before God, he has to live upon the daily charity of the Most High; therefore, what can he have to give to me? Oh, do not look to your fellow virgins for the oil of grace, for they do not have enough for themselves and you. (See Matthew 25:1–13.) Whatever name a man may dare to take, whether it is priest, father, or Pope, do not look to him, but look to Jesus, in whom all fullness dwells (Col. 1:19).

The glory that overflows to Christ from our daily dependence is seen in His becoming to us our daily bread. His flesh is meat indeed, His blood is drink indeed (John 6:55), and we must feed upon these continually or die. Eating is not an operation to be performed only once, but it is to be done throughout life. Likewise, we have to go to Jesus again and again and find sustenance in Him as long as life lasts.

Dear readers, we honored our Lord at first when He saved us, and we are led to honor Him every day by being daily dependent upon Him. If we are right in our hearts, we will honor Him more and more every day, as we more and more perceive our indebtedness to Him. He is our daily bread on which we feed continually, and the living water of which we drink continually. He is the light that everlastingly shines upon us. He is, in fact, our all in all, and all this prevents us from forgetting Him. As He saved us at the first, so He saves us still; as we prized Him at the first, we prize Him still.

More than that, as our lives are maintained not only by Him, but also by our abiding in union with Him, this leads us to abide in love toward Him. Union is the source of communion and love. The wife remains a happy wife through a loving fellowship with her husband. When the betrothed one is married to her beloved, the wedding day is not the end of it all; the putting on of the ring is the beginning, not the end. And so, when we believe in Jesus, we are saved, but we must not idly feel that "it is all done now." No, it has only begun. The life of dependence, the life of faith, the life of obedience, the life of love, the life of union has now begun, and it is to be continued forever. This makes us love, honor, and adore our Lord Jesus, since we only live by being one with Him.

We must also remember that our lives are daily supported by virtue of what the living Redeemer is still doing for us, as well as by receiving the fruit of His death and our spiritual union with Him. *"He ever liveth to make intercession for* [us]," and, therefore, He is *"able also to save them to the uttermost that come unto God by him"* (Heb. 7:25). The life of the ascended Redeemer is intimately bound up with our lives: *"Because I live, ye shall live also"* (John 14:19). This honors Christ, for we are thus led to conceive of a living Savior and to love Him as a living, breathing, acting person.

It is a pity when men only think of a dead Savior or of a baby Savior, carried in the Virgin's arms, as the church of Rome does. It is our joy to have a living Christ, for while He lives we cannot die, and while He pleads we cannot be condemned. Thus, we are led to remember Him as a living Savior and to give Him honor.

But, oh, my fellow Christians, how great the fullness of Christ must be! All the grace that the saints have must come out of Him. It is not merely that all they have had has come from Him, but all they obtain every day also comes from Him. If there is any virtue, if there is any praise, if there is anything heavenly, if there is anything divine, we have received it out of His fullness *"and grace for grace"* (John 1:16).

How great must that power be that protects and preserves myriads of saints from temptation and keeps them amid perils as many as the sands of the sea! How great must that patience be that watches over the frail children of God in all their weaknesses and wanderings, in all their sufferings, in all their infirmities! How great must His grace be, which covers all their sin, and how great must His strength be, which supports them under all their trials! How great must the Fountainhead be, when the streams that flow to any one of us are so deep that we cannot fathom them, so broad that we cannot measure them!

Millions of happy spirits are each receiving as much as any one of us may be receiving, and still there is a fullness abiding in Christ that is the same as before, for it has pleased the Father that in Him should all fullness dwell (Col. 1:19). Not even one saint lives a moment apart from Him, for *"none can keep alive his own soul."*

The cries of babes in grace and the shouts of strong men who divide the spoil (Matt. 12:29) all come from the life that He lends and the strength that He gives. Between the gates of hell and the gates of heaven, in all those pilgrims whose faces are turned toward the royal city, all the life is Christ's life, and all the strength is Christ's strength. He is in them, working in them to will and to do of His own good pleasure (Phil. 2:13). Blessed be the name of the Lord Jesus, who thus supplies all His people. Does this not display the exceeding riches of His grace?

The Path of Wisdom

Thirdly, this subject suggests the path of wisdom for us. If *"none can keep alive his own soul,"* then what kind of people should we be?

I hope that you will earnestly think about this for a few moments. Do not allow yourself to look back to a certain day and say, "On that occasion I was regenerated and converted, and that is enough." I am afraid that some of you get into a very bad condition by saying, "If I can prove that I was converted on such and such a day, that will be enough." This is altogether unjustifiable. Conversion is a turning onto the right road. The next thing to do is to walk on it. The daily progression along that road is as essential as the beginning, if you hope to reach the desired end.

To start in the race is nothing. Many who have done that have failed. But to hold out until you reach the finish line is the whole test of the matter. To strike the first blow is not the entire battle; the victory is promised to him who overcomes. (See Revelation 3:21.) Perseverance is as necessary to a man's salvation as conversion is. Remember, not only do you need grace to begin with, but also grace with which you may abide in Christ Jesus.

Let this be a lesson to us, that we should diligently use all those means whereby the Lord communicates fresh support to our lives. A man does not say, "Well, I was born on such and such a day; that is enough for me." No, the man needs his daily meals to maintain a healthy existence. Being alive, his next consideration is to stay alive, and, therefore, he does not neglect eating or any operation that is essential to life. Likewise, dear friends, you must labor for the meat that endures to eternal life (John 6:27); you must feed on the Bread of Heaven.

Study the Scriptures daily—I hope you do not neglect that. Be much in private prayer; your life cannot be healthy if the mercy seat is neglected. Do not forsake the assembling of yourselves together, as the manner of some is (Heb. 10:25). Be eager to hear the Word, and endeavor both to understand and to practice it. Gather with God's people in their spiritual meetings when they join in prayer and praise, for these are healthy means of sustaining the inner life. If you neglect these, you cannot expect that grace will be strong within you. You may even question if there is any life at all.

Remember, even if a man eats and drinks, that would not keep him alive without the power of God, and many die when there is a great supply of air, food, and water. You must, therefore, look beyond outward means to God Himself to preserve your soul. And let this be your daily prayer: "O Savior, by whom I began to live, daily enable me to look to You, so that I may draw continuous life from Your wounds, and live because You live." Take these things into your heart and practice them.

Also, keep clear of everything that has a tendency to destroy life. A sane man does not willingly take poison; if he knew it was poison, he would not touch the cup that had been tainted. We are careful to avoid any adulteration in our food that might be injurious to life and health. We have our chemists busily at work to analyze liquids, lest we should inadvertently take in death in the water that we drink.

Believers, let us now be equally careful about our souls. Keep your "chemist" at work analyzing the things of this life. Let conscience and understanding equip their laboratory and prove all things. Analyze the sermon of the eloquent preacher, lest you should drink in novelties of doctrine and complete falsehoods, because he happens to put them prettily before you. Analyze each book you read, lest you should become tainted with error while you are interested in the style and manner, the smartness and elegance of the author. Analyze the company you keep; test and try everything, lest you should by chance be committing spiritual suicide or carelessly squandering life away. Ask the Lord, the preserver of men, above all things, to keep you beneath the shadow of His wings, so that you may not be afraid *"for the pestilence that walketh in darkness; nor for the destruction that wasteth at noonday"* (Ps. 91:6), because His truth has become your shield, and you are safe.

Watch your life carefully, but look to Jesus Christ from day to day for everything. Do not become self-satisfied, so as to say, *"I am rich, and increased with goods"* (Rev. 3:17). If ever a child of God imitates the rich man in the parable and says, *"Soul, thou hast much goods laid up for many years; take thine ease"* (Luke 12:19), he is a fool as much as the rich man was.

I have known some people who have become very exalted in spiritual things. They can hardly remember having been convicted, temptation has no power over them, they are masters of the situation, and their condition is of the most elevated kind. Well, riding in a hot air balloon is very pleasant for some people, but I think it is safest to stay on the ground.

Likewise, I fear that "spiritual ballooning" has been very harmful to a great many and has turned their heads entirely away from what should be their primary focus.

Their high opinions of themselves are falsehoods. After all, my friend, although you think you are better than other people, you are in fact no better, and the one area in which I am sure you miserably fail is in humility. When we hear you declare what a fine person you are, we suspect that the feathers in your cap are borrowed and that you are not what you seem. A peacock is a beautiful bird; what can be more brilliant? But none of us is delighted by his voice. Similarly, certain people may have many fine feathers—perhaps a little too fine—but while they are showing themselves off, we know that they have a weak area, and we pray that it may not cause dishonor to the name of Christ.

It is not our duty to be hunting about for the failings of our fellow Christians, yet boasting has a tendency to make us examine the boaster. The practical thing is to believe that when we ourselves are proud, there is something wrong. Whenever we stand before the mirror and think what fine people we are, we had better go at once to the Great Physician and beg Him to give us medicine for our vanity. Mr. Peacock, you are certainly very handsome, but you should hear yourself croak. Mr. Professor of Faith, there are many fine points about you, but there are sorry ones, too; so be humble and therefore wise. Brother, if you get an inch above the ground, you are an inch too high.

If you have anything apart from Christ, if you can live five minutes on past experience, if you think you can live on yesterday's grace, you make a mistake. You so cleverly set aside the manna; you stored it up in the cupboard with such self-content. Go to it tomorrow morning instead of joining the rest of your fellow Christians in gathering the fresh manna that will fall all around the camp. Go to the cupboard where you stored up yesterday's manna! Ah, as soon as you open the door, you close it again. Why do you shut that door so speedily? Well, we do not need to look inside the cupboard; the smell is enough. It has happened as Moses foretold it; it has bred worms, and it stinks as he said it would. Cover it up as quickly as you can. Dig a deep hole, throw it all in, and bury it; that is the only thing to do with such rottenness.

Go to Christ day by day, and you will get your manna sweet, but begin to live on past or present attainments, and they will breed worms and stink as surely as you are human. Remember, *"none can keep alive his own soul."*

A Way to Serve God

Last of all, this subject indicates a way of usefulness for everyone who is a child of God. I think the great business of the Christian's life is to serve God, and he can do that mainly by aiming at the conversion of sinners. It is a grand thing to be used by God to turn sinners from the error of their ways, but, my friends, there is equally good work to be done by helping struggling saints.

In the days of the old Roman empire, a Roman would say he thought it as much an honor to preserve a Roman citizen as to slay an enemy of his country, and he was right. Likewise, there is as much acceptance before God in the work of preserving souls alive as in being the means of making souls live in the first place. In other words, the *upholding* of believers is as necessary an exercise for Christian workers as the *ingathering* of unbelievers.

I want you to think about this. If someone is nearly drowned, a man will leap into the water to bring him out, and he gets great credit for it, which he deserves. And so, when a man saves a soul from death by earnest ministry, let him be glad and thank God. But if a man is starving and ready to die and you give him bread, or if he is not reduced to that point but would have been so had you not interfered, then you have done as good an action in preserving life as the other man who snatched life from between the jaws of death. You must never think little of the work that instructs the ignorant Christian, that clears the stumbling blocks out of the way of the perplexed believer, that comforts the feebleminded, and that supports the weak. These works must be done, while soulwinning must not be left undone.

Perhaps some of you will never be the means of the conversion of many. In that case, then, try to be the means of comfort to as many as you can. To be the means of nurturing the life that God has given is a worthy service and is very acceptable with God. I would urge the members of every church to watch over one another. Be pastors to each other. Be very concerned about the many young people who are among you. If you see any backslide, in a gentle and affectionate manner endeavor to bring them back.

Do you know anyone who is despondent or depressed? Spend some of your time in comforting him. Do you see faults in anyone you know? Do not tell him of them hastily, but allow God to work through you to teach him a better way. Just as the Lord often preserves you by the help of others, so, in return, seek to be the means by which He will keep your brothers and sisters from going astray, from sinking in despair, or from falling into error. I present it to you as a good and blessed work to do—will you try to accomplish it?

Now, if you say yes—and I think you do say yes—then I must write to you *"concerning the collection for the saints"* (1 Cor. 16:1). Do you see any connection between this subject and the collection? I know I do. We must contribute our full share. Many who are ill will die unless they are carefully looked after, unless medicine and a physician's skill are provided for them. I hope I have brought you to the place where you are ready enough to look after sick souls. Well, he who would look after a sick soul will surely be ready to care for a sick body.

I hope you are not of the same class as the priest in the fable who was entreated by a beggar to give him a crown, which is worth five shillings. "By no means," said the reverend father, "why should I give you a crown?" "Will you give me a shilling, holy father?" No, he would not give him a shilling, nor even a penny. "Then," said he, "holy father, will you of your charity give me a farthing?" This had the value of one fourth of a penny. No, he would not do anything of the sort. At last the beggar said, "Would not your reverence be kind enough to give me your blessing?" "Oh yes, my son, you shall have it at once; kneel down and receive it." But the man did not kneel down to receive it, for he reasoned that if the blessing had been worth a farthing, the holy father would not have given it to him, and so he went his way.

Men always have enough practical sense to determine that if professed Christians do not care for their bodily needs, there cannot be much sincerity in their zeal for men's souls. If a man will give me spiritual bread in the form of a tract but will not give me a piece of bread for my body, how can I think much of him? Practical help to the poor must accompany the spiritual help that you give them. If you wish to help to keep a brother's soul alive in the higher sense, do not be unwilling to do it in the more ordinary way. Take every opportunity to prove your sincerity and to gratify your charity by contributing your money in addition to your service.

Chapter 2

Christ, the Tree of Life

In the midst of the street of it, and on either side of the river, was there the tree of life, which bare twelve manner of fruits, and yielded her fruit every month: and the leaves of the tree were for the healing of the nations.
—Revelation 22:2

We saw in the first chapter that "*none can keep alive his own soul*" (Ps. 22:29) and that our spiritual lives must be sustained by God. It is so necessary in the Christian life to look every day to Jesus Christ for everything. Christ is to be our Tree of Life, the One we go to for our sustenance and for our strength. With this in mind, let us now look in this chapter at the place Christ takes as our Tree of Life.

You will remember that, in the first Paradise, there was a tree of life in the midst of the Garden. When Adam had sinned and was driven out, God said,

> *Lest he put forth his hand, and take also of the tree of life, and eat, and live for ever: therefore the LORD God...drove out the man.* (Gen. 3:22–24)

It has been supposed, by some, that this tree of life in the Garden of Eden was intended to be the means of giving man his immortality, that his feeding upon it would have supported him in the vigor of unfailing youth, preserved him from exposure to decay, and imparted to his nature the seal of perpetuity by a spiritual regeneration. I do not know about that. But if it were so, I can understand the reason why God would not allow the first man, Adam, to become immortal in the lapsed state he was then in. Instead, God ordained that the old nature should die and that the immortality should be given to a new nature, which would be formed under another leadership and quickened by another Spirit.

Our text tells us that, in the center of the new paradise—in the perfect paradise of God from which the saints will never be driven, as it is to be our perpetual heritage—there is also a Tree of Life. But here we see it as a metaphor; we do not understand that tree to be literal. I believe our Lord Jesus Christ to be none other than that Tree of Life, whose leaves are *"for the healing of the nations."* I can hardly imagine any other interpretation, for this seems to me to be so full of meaning and to give such unspeakable satisfaction.

At any rate, if this is not the absolute purpose of the sublime vision that John saw, it is most certainly true that our Lord Jesus Christ is life from the dead, and life to His own living people. He is all in all to them. By Him, and by Him alone, must their spiritual life be maintained. We are right enough, then, in saying that Jesus Christ is a Tree of Life, and we will so speak of Him in the hope that some may come and pluck His fruit, and eat and live forever. Perhaps by this sacred allegory, some poor, dying soul may be encouraged to take hold of eternal life by laying hold of Jesus Christ.

First, in this allegory, we will study the Tree of Life in the winter, when no fruit can be found on it. Secondly, we will study the Tree of Life as it is budding and blossoming. Thirdly, we will study the way in which we may partake of its fruits.

The Tree of Life in the Wintertime

First of all, let us think of Jesus Christ, the Tree of Life, in the wintertime. You might immediately think, and rightly so, that by this illustration I intend to describe Jesus in His sufferings, in His dark wintry days, when He hung upon the cross, bled, and died; when He had no honor from men and no respect from anyone; when even God the Father hid His face from Him for a season, and He was made sin for us, that we might be made the righteousness of God in Him (2 Cor. 5:21). It is true, my dear friends, that you will never see the Tree of Life in the right way unless you first look at the cross. It was there that this Tree gathered strength to bring forth its after-fruit. It was there that Jesus Christ, by His glorious merits and His wondrous work achieved upon the cross, obtained power to become the Redeemer of our souls and the Captain of our salvation.

Come with me, then, by faith, to the foot of the little mound of Calvary, and let us look up and see this thing that came to pass. Let us turn aside, as Moses did when the bush burned, and see this great sight. It is the greatest marvel that ever earth or hell or heaven beheld, and we may well spend a few minutes in beholding it.

Our Lord Jesus, the Ever Living, the Immortal, the Eternal, became man, *"and being found in fashion as a man, he humbled himself, and* [died]...*the death of the cross"* (Phil. 2:8). That death was not on His own account. His humanity had no need to die. He might have lived on and have seen no death, if He had so willed. He had committed no offense, no sin, and, therefore, no punishment could fall upon Him.

For sins not his own
He died to atone.

Every pang upon the cross was substitutionary; for you, the sons of men, the Prince of Glory bled, *"the just for the unjust, that he might bring us to God"* (1 Pet. 3:18). His pain was not the result of anything He had done, for the Father loved Him with an ineffable love, and He deserved no blows from His Father's hand. But His pains were for the sins of His enemies, for your sins and mine, that by His stripes we might be healed (Isa. 53:5) and that through His wounds reconciliation might be made with God.

An Accursed Death

Think, then, of the Savior's death upon the cross. Take careful notice that it was an accursed death. There were many ways by which men might die, but there was only one death that God pronounced to be accursed. He did not say, "Cursed is he who dies by stoning, or by the sword, or by a millstone being fastened about his neck, or by being eaten by worms," but it was written, *"He that is hanged is accursed of God"* (Deut. 21:23), and, *"Cursed is every one that hangeth on a tree"* (Gal. 3:13). By no other death than that one, which God singled out as the death of the accursed, could Jesus Christ die. Admire this fact, believer, that Jesus Christ was made a curse for us. Admire, and love; let your faith and your gratitude blend together.

A Shameful Death

Christ suffered a death of the most ignominious kind. The Roman law subjected only felons to it, and, I believe, not even felons unless they were slaves. Neither a freed Roman nor a subject of any of the kingdoms that Rome had conquered had any chance of ever dying in this way, but only the slave who was bought and sold in the market could be put to this kind of death. The Jews counted Jesus worthy to be sold as a slave, and then they put Him to a slave's death for you.

A Ridiculed Death

Besides this, they added their own ridicule to the natural scorn of the death. Some passed by and shook their heads. Some stood still and thrust out their tongues at Him; others sat down, watched Him there, and satisfied their malice and their scorn. He was made the center of all sorts of ridicule and shame. He was the drunkard's song, and even those who were crucified with Him reviled Him. And all this He suffered for us. Our sin was shameful, and He was made to be a shame for us. We had disgraced ourselves and had dishonored God, and, therefore, Jesus was joined with the wicked in His death and made as vile as they.

A Painful Death

The death was also exceedingly painful. We must not forget the pangs of the Savior's body, for I believe that when we begin to depreciate the physical sufferings, we very soon begin to drag down the spiritual sufferings, too. It must be a fearful death by which to die, when the tender hands and feet are pierced, when the bones are dislocated by the jarring that comes as the cross is erected, when the fever sets in, when the mouth becomes hot as an oven, the tongue is swollen in the mouth, and the only moisture given is vinegar mingled with gall. Ah, beloved! None of us can guess the pangs that Jesus knew. We believe that Hart described it well when he said that Christ bore

> All that incarnate God could bear,
> With strength enough, and none to spare.

You cannot tell the price of griefs and groans, heartbreakings and soul-tearings, sighs and rendings of the spirit, which Jesus had to pay so that He might redeem us from our iniquities.

A Lingering Death

It was a lingering death. However painful a death may be, it is always some comfort to think that it will soon be over. When a man is hanged or beheaded, the pain may be great for the instant, but it is soon over and gone. But in crucifixion, a man lives so long that when Pilate heard the Savior was dead, he marveled that He had already died (Mark 15:44). I remember hearing a missionary say that he saw a man crucified in Burma and that he was alive two days after having been nailed to the cross. I believe there are authenticated stories of people who have been taken down from the cross after having hung for forty-eight hours and, after all that, have had their wounds healed and have lived for years. It was a lingering death that the Savior had to die.

Oh, my dear friends, if you put these items together, they make up a ghastly total, which ought to press upon our hearts. If we are believers, such thoughts ought to stir up grateful affection. And if we are unbelievers, we ought to be provoked to shame that we do not love Him who loved the sons of men so much.

A Death of Punishment

The death of the Lord Jesus Christ for us, I must also add, was penal. He died the death of the condemned. Perhaps most men would feel this is the worst feature; for, if a man dies a painful death but it is accidental, it does not have the sting that comes with it if the death is caused by law, and especially if it is brought about by sin. Now, our Lord Jesus Christ was condemned to die by both the civil and ecclesiastical officials of the country. And what was more, *"it pleased the LORD to bruise him; he hath put him to grief"* (Isa. 53:10). Jesus Christ died without any sin of His own, yet He died a penal death, because our sins were counted as

His. He took upon Himself our iniquities as though they were His own, and then, being found in the sinner's place, He suffered the wrath and punishment that were due for sin as if He had been a sinner.

A Hopeful Death

Beloved Christians, I wish it were in my power to set forth Christ crucified—Christ visibly crucified—among you! Oh, I wish I could paint such a picture of Him that the eyes of your hearts could see Him! I wish that I could make you feel the anguish of His grief and sip that bitter cup that He had to drain to the dregs. But if I cannot do this, it will suffice me to say that *His death is the only hope for sinners.* Those wounds of His are the gates to heaven. The pains and sufferings of Immanuel are the only atoning sacrifice for human guilt. Oh, you who would be saved, turn your eyes to Him! *"Look unto* [Him], *and be ye saved, all the ends of the earth"* (Isa. 45:22). There is life in just looking at Him; there is life nowhere else. Despise Him, and you perish. Accept Him, and you will never perish, neither will all the powers of hell prevail against you.

Come, guilty souls! Jesus does not want your tears or your blood. His tears can cleanse you; His blood can purify you. If your heart is not as broken as you wish it would be, it is His broken heart, not yours, that will gain heaven for you. If you cannot be what you desire to be, He was—for you—what God would have Him to be. God is contented with Him, so you also may be contented with Him. Simply come and trust Him. Oh, may all the delays be past, and all the difficulties be solved, and just as you are, without one plea but that the Savior bled, come to your heavenly Father, and you will be *"accepted in the beloved"* (Eph. 1:6).

In this way, then, Jesus Christ hanging on the cross is the Tree of Life in its wintertime. And now let me show you, as far as I am able, that Tree of Life when it had blossomed and brought forth fruit.

The Tree Blossoms and Bears Fruit

There He stands—Jesus, still the same Jesus—and yet how changed! The same Jesus, but clothed with honor instead of shame, able now to save them to the uttermost that come unto God by Him (Heb. 7:25). My text says of this tree that it bears *"twelve manner of fruits."* I suppose that is intended to signify that a perfect and complete assortment of supplies for all human necessities is to be found in Christ—all sorts of mercies for all sorts of sinners, all kinds of blessings to suit all kinds of needs.

We know that every bit of the palm tree is useful, from its root to its fruit. So is it with the Lord Jesus Christ. There is nothing in Him that we could afford to do without. There is nothing about Jesus that is extraneous or superfluous. You can put Him to use in every part of life, in every sort of employment, in every kind of relationship.

Spiritual Food

A tree of life is for food. Some trees yield rich fruit. Adam in the Garden lived only on the fruit of the Garden. Jesus Christ is the food of His people, and what delicious food they have! What satisfying food, what plenteous food, what sweet food, what food precisely suitable to all the needs of their souls, Jesus is! As for manna, it was angels' food; but what will I say of Christ? He is more than that, for

> Never did angels taste above,
> Redeeming grace and dying love.

Oh, how richly you are fed! The flesh of God's own Son is the spiritual food of every heir of heaven. Hungry souls, come to Jesus if you wish to be fed.

Spiritual Drink

Jesus also gives His people drink. There are some tropical trees that, as soon as they are tapped, yield liquids as sweet and rich as milk, and many people drink and are refreshed by them. Jesus Christ's blood is the wine of His people. The atonement that He has perfected by His sufferings is the golden cup out of which they drink and drink again, until their mourning souls are made glad, until their fainting hearts are strengthened and refreshed. Jesus gives us the water of life, the "*wines on the lees well refined*" (Isa. 25:6), the "*wine and milk without money and without price*" (Isa. 55:1). What a Tree of Life, to yield us both food and drink!

Clothing for the Soul

Jesus is our Tree of Life yielding clothing, too. Adam went to the fig tree for his garments, and the fig leaves yielded him such covering as they could. But we come to Christ, and we find not fig leaves, but a robe of righteousness (Isa. 61:10) that is matchless for its beauty, comely in its proportions, one that will never wear out, that exactly suits to cover our nakedness from head to foot. When we put it on, it makes us fair to look upon, even as Christ Himself. Oh, you who desire to be rearrayed until you are fit to stand among the royal attendants of the skies, come to Jesus, and find upon this Tree of Life the garments that you need!

Soul Medicine

This Tree also yields medicine. *"The leaves of the tree were for the healing of the nations."* Lay a plaster upon any wound, and if it is but the plaster of King Jesus, it will heal the wound. Just one promise from His lips, just one leaf from this Tree, just one word from His Spirit, just one drop of His blood, and this is heaven's plaster indeed. It is true that there was no balm in Gilead; there was no physician there. Therefore, the wound of the daughter of the people of Israel was not healed. (See Jeremiah 8:22.) But there is balm in Jesus, there is a Physician at Calvary, and the wound of the daughter of God's people will be healed if she will but run to Jesus Christ for healing.

A Shelter from the Storm

And what more can be said? Is there anything else that your spirits can need? O children of God, Christ is all! O ungodly ones, who have been roaming through the wood to find the tree that would supply your needs, stop here. This *"apple tree among the trees of the wood"* (Song 2:3) is the Tree that your souls require. Stay here, and you will have all that you need. This Tree yields a shelter from the storm. Other trees are dangerous when the tempest howls; but he who shelters beneath the tree of the Lord Jesus will find that all the thunderbolts of God will fly by him and do him no injury. He who clings to Jesus cannot be hurt.

Heaven and earth would sooner pass away than a soul be lost who hides beneath the boughs of this Tree. And oh, you who have hidden there to shelter from the wrath of God, let me remind you that in every other kind of danger it will also yield you shelter. And if you are not in danger, still in the hot days of care you will find the shade of it to be cool and genial. The spouse in Solomon's Song said, *"I sat down under his shadow with great delight, and his fruit was sweet to my taste"* (Song 2:3). If you have Christ, you will have comfort, joy, peace, and liberty; and when the trouble comes, you will find shelter and deliverance by coming near to Him.

He is the Tree of Life, then, yielding twelve different kinds of fruits. Those fruits are always ripe and always ready, for they ripen every month, and they are free to everyone who desires them. The leaves are not for the healing of only some but *"for the healing of the nations."* What a meaningful passage of Scripture! There are enough of these leaves for the healing of all the nations that will ever come into the world. Oh, may God grant that none of you may die from spiritual sickness when these leaves can heal you, and may none of you be filling yourselves with the sour grapes of this world, the poisonous grapes of sin, while the sweet fruits of Christ's love are waiting, which would refresh you and satisfy you.

How to Get the Fruit

And now I have to show you how to partake of the fruit of this Tree of Life. That is the most important point. It profits you little for me to tell you that there is fruit, unless I can tell you how it can be obtained. Dear readers, it is my wish that you really desire to know the way, but I am afraid that many care very little about it. A learned pastor had once been out to tea with a member of his congregation who had been particularly hospitable to him, and when he was leaving, he said, "Well, now, madam, you have treated me exceedingly well, but how do you treat my Master?" That is a question I would like to ask some of you. How do you treat my Master? Why, you treat Him as if He were not Christ, as if you did not need Him at all. But you do need Him, and may you find Him soon. When you come to die, you will need Him then, and perhaps then you may not find Him.

By Faith

Well, the first way to get the fruit from this Tree is by faith. That is the hand that plucks the golden apples. Can you believe? That is the important thing. Can you believe that Jesus is the Son of God, that He died upon the cross? "Yes," you say, "I believe that." Can you believe that, in consequence of His sufferings, He is able to save? "Yes," you say. Can you believe that He will save you? Will you trust Him to save you? If so, you are saved. If your soul comes to Jesus and says, "My Lord, I believe in You, that You are able to save to the uttermost, and now I throw myself upon You," that is faith.

When Andrew Fuller was going to preach before a group of people, he rode to the meeting on his horse. There had been a good deal of rain, and the rivers were very high. He got to one river that he had to cross. He looked at it, and he was half afraid of the strong current, because he did not know how deep it was. A farmer, who happened to be standing nearby, said to him, "It is all right, Mr. Fuller. You will get through it all right, sir; the horse will keep its footing." Mr. Fuller went in, and the water got up to the saddle strap, and then up to the saddle, and he began to get uncomfortably wet. Mr. Fuller thought he had better turn around, and he was going to do so when the same farmer shouted, "Go on, Mr. Fuller, go on. I know it is all right." And Mr. Fuller said, "Then I will go on; I will go by faith."

Now, sinner, it is very much like that with you. You think that your sins are so deep that Christ will never be able to carry you over them. But I say to you: It is all right, sinner; trust Jesus, and He will carry you through hell itself, if that is necessary. If all the sins of all the men who have ever lived were all yours, if you could trust Him, Jesus Christ would carry you through the current of all that sin. It is all right! Only trust Christ. The river may be deep, but Christ's love is deeper still. It is all right!

Do not let the Devil make you doubt my Lord and Master. The Devil has been a liar from the beginning and the father of lies (John 8:44), but my Master is *"Faithful and True"*

(Rev. 19:11). Rely on Him, and all will be well. The waves may roll; the river may seem to be deeper than you thought it to be—and rest assured it is much deeper than you know it to be. But the almighty arm of Jesus—that strong arm that can shake the heavens and the earth and move the pillars thereof (see Job 9:4, 6) as Samson moved the pillar of Gaza's gates—that strong arm can hold you up and bear you safely through, if you will but cling to it and rest on it. O soul, rest in Jesus, and you may know that you are saved!

By Prayer

Secondly, if you do not seem to get the fruit from this Tree by faith, shake it by prayer. "Oh!" you say, "I have been praying." Yes, but a tree does not always drop its fruit at the first shake you give it. Shake it again, and then give it another shake! Sometimes, when the tree is loaded and is pretty firm in the earth, you have to shake it to and fro, and finally you have to plant your feet, get a firm hold of it, and shake it with all your might, until you strain every muscle and sinew, in order to get the fruit down. And that is the way to pray. Shake the Tree of Life until mercy drops into your lap.

Christ loves for men to strenuously plead with Him. You cannot be too persistent in your asking. That which might be disagreeable to your fellowmen, when you beg of them, will be agreeable to Christ. Oh, go to your prayer chamber; get yourself to your prayer closet, you who have not found Christ. Get to your bedside, to your little closet, and *"seek ye the LORD while he may be found, call ye upon him while he is near"* (Isa. 55:6).

May the Spirit of God constrain you to pray. May He constrain you to continue in prayer. Jesus will have to hear you. The gate of heaven is open to the sturdy knocker who will not take a denial. May the Lord enable you to so plead that, in the end, you will be able to say, "You have heard my voice and my supplications. You have inclined Your ear unto me. Therefore, I will pray unto You as long as I live." (See Psalm 116:1–2.)

May God add His blessing to these thoughts, for Jesus' sake! Amen.

Chapter 3

Our Lord's Preaching

The LORD hath anointed me to preach good tidings unto the meek; he hath sent me to bind up the brokenhearted.
—Isaiah 61:1

You will remember how, in chapter two, I said that Christ, the Tree of Life, is like a medicine to His people. Revelation 22:2 says, *"The leaves of the tree were for the healing of the nations."* Jesus is our Great Physician, the Healer of all who will come to Him. From the Scriptures we know that He is the Balm of Gilead, and all our hurts can be soothed and healed by His touch.

The ministry of Jesus upon this earth was the means by which God brought such healing and relief to us. And what was that ministry? It was a ministry of preaching. Our Lord was especially anointed to preach. The Lord of heaven and earth attaches so much honor to the ministry of the Word that, as one of the old Puritans said, "God had only one Son, and He made a preacher of Him." It would greatly encourage the weakest among us who are preachers of righteousness to think that the Son of God, the blessed and eternal Word, came into this world so that He might preach the same glad tidings that we are called to proclaim. Let us now look in greater detail at our Lord's ministry of preaching.

A Constant Sermon

Throughout His ministry, our Lord earnestly kept to His work. It was His business to preach, and He did preach. In fact, He was always preaching. "What," you ask, "did He not also work miracles?" Yes, but His miracles were sermons; they were discourses acted out, full of instruction. He preached when He was on the mountain; He equally preached when He sat for a meal in the Pharisee's house. All His actions were significant; He preached by every movement. He preached when He did not speak; His silence was as eloquent as His words. He preached when He gave, and He preached when He received. He was preaching a sermon when He lent His feet to the woman so that she could wash them with her tears and wipe them with the hairs of her head (see Luke 7:37–38), quite as much as when He was dividing the loaves and the fishes and feeding the multitude. (See Matthew 14:15–21.) He preached by His patience before Pilate, for there He made a good confession (1 Tim. 6:13). He preached from the bloody tree; with hands and feet fastened there, He delivered the most wonderful discourse of justice and of love, of vengeance and of grace, of death and of life, that was ever preached in this poor world.

Yes, He preached wondrously, and He was always preaching. With all His heart and soul He preached! He prayed so that He might obtain strength to preach. He wept in secret, so that He might the more compassionately speak the Word, which wipes men's tears away. Always a preacher, He was always ready with a good word, in season and out of season (2 Tim. 4:2). As He walked the streets, He preached as He went. If He sought retirement and the people thronged Him, He did not send them away without a gracious word.

This was His one calling, and this one calling He pursued in the power of the eternal Spirit. He liked it so well and thought so much of it that He trained His eleven friends to do the same work, sending them out to preach as He had done. (See Luke 9:1–6.) Then He chose seventy more disciples to go on the same errand. (See Luke 10:1–17.) Did He shave the head of even one of them to make him a priest? Did He decorate any of them with ceremonial robes or caps? Did He teach any one of them to say mass, to swing a censer, or to elevate the host? Did He instruct any one of them to regenerate children by baptism? Did He bring them up to chant in loose, white garments and march in procession? No, those things He never thought of, and neither will we.

If He had thought of them, it would only have been with utter contempt, for what is there in such childish things? The preaching of the Cross is foolishness to them that perish, but unto us who are saved it is the wisdom and the power of God (1 Cor. 1:18, 23–24). It pleases God still *"by the foolishness of preaching to save them that believe"* (v. 21).

Neither had our Lord lowered His estimate of preaching at the close of His career. Just before He ascended, He said, *"Go ye into all the world, and preach the gospel to every creature"* (Mark 16:15). His last charge, in brief, was, "Preach; preach even as I have done before you." He lived as the Prince of preachers; He died and became the theme of preachers; He lives again and is the Lord of preachers. What an honorable work is that to which His servants are called!

Good Tidings

Now that you have seen that our Savior came to preach, notice His subject: *"The Lord hath anointed me to preach good tidings unto the meek."*

And what good tidings did He preach? Pardon—pardon given to the chief of sinners; pardon for prodigal sons held tightly to their Father's bosom. He preached to sinners the good tidings of restoration from their lost estate, as a piece of money that is restored to the treasury and a lost sheep that is brought back to the fold. How encouragingly He preached of life given to men dead in sin, life through the living water that becomes a fountain within the soul! (See John 7:38.)

How sweetly He would say, *"He that believeth on the Son hath everlasting life"* (John 3:36); *"He that believeth in me, though he were dead, yet shall he live"* (John 11:25); *"As Moses lifted up the serpent in the wilderness, even so must the Son of man be lifted up: that whosoever believeth in him should not perish, but have eternal life"* (John 3:14–15). He preached the absolute necessity of having a change of heart and the need for becoming a new creation. He said, *"Ye must be born again"* (v. 7), and He taught those truths by which the Holy Spirit works in us and makes all things new.

He preached glad tidings concerning resurrection and entreated men to look for endless bliss by faith in Him. He cried, *"I am the resurrection, and the life...and whosoever liveth and believeth in me shall never die"* (John 11:25–26). He gave forth precepts, too, and threats in their place—some of them very searching and terrible—but they were only used as accessories to the Good News. He made men feel that they were poor, so that they might be willing to be made rich by His grace. He made them feel weary and burdened, so that they might come to Him for rest. But the sum and substance of what He preached was the Gospel, the "good spell" as it was originally called, the glad news.

Fellow believers, our divine Lord always preached upon that subject and did not stoop to secular themes. If you notice, though, He would sometimes debate with Pharisees, Herodians, and others, as it became necessary. Yet He was soon away from them and back to His one theme. He baffled them with His wisdom and then returned to the work He loved, namely, preaching where the publicans and sinners drew near together *"to hear him"* (Luke 15:1).

Our business, since the Spirit of God is upon us, is not to teach politics, except insofar as it immediately touches the kingdom of Christ, and there the Gospel is the best weapon. Nor is it our business to be preaching mere morals and rules of duty; our ethics must be drawn from the Cross and begin and end there. Our task is not so much to declare what men ought to do, as it is to preach the good news of what God has done for them. Nor must we always be preaching certain doctrines as mere doctrines, apart from Christ. We are only theologians as far as theology enshrines the Gospel. We have one thing to do, and to that one thing we must keep. The old proverb said, "Cobbler, stick to your last." Believe me, that is good advice to the Christian minister—to stick to the Gospel and make no move away from it.

I hope I have always kept to my subject; but I take no credit for it, for I know nothing else. Like the apostle Paul, I have determined not to know anything among men, except *"Jesus Christ, and him crucified"* (1 Cor. 2:2). Indeed, *"necessity is laid upon me; yea, woe is unto me, if I preach not the gospel"* (1 Cor. 9:16).

I would willingly have only one eye, and that eye capable of seeing nothing from the pulpit except lost men and the Gospel of their salvation. To all else I may as well be blind, so that the entire force of my mind may center on the great essential subject. There is certainly enough in the Gospel for any one man, enough to fill any one life, to absorb all thought, emotion, desire, and energy; yes, infinitely more than the most experienced Christian and the most intelligent teacher will ever be able to bring forth.

If our Master kept to His one topic, we may wisely do the same. If anyone says that we are narrow, let us delight in that blessed narrowness, which brings men into the narrow way (Matt. 7:14). If anyone denounces us as being cramped in our ideas and being confined to one set of truths, let us rejoice to be confined with Christ and consider it the truest enlargement of our minds. We would do well to be bound with cords to His altar, to lose all hearing but for His voice, all seeing but for His light, all life but in His life, all glorying but in His Cross. If He who knew all things taught only the one thing that is needed (Luke 10:42), His servants may rightly enough do the same. *"The LORD hath anointed me,"* He says, *"to preach good tidings."* In this anointing let us abide.

Encouragement for the Meek

Now notice the people to whom He especially addressed the good tidings. They were *"the meek."* Just look in the New Testament where our Lord was reading this passage from the book of Isaiah in the synagogue at Nazareth, and you will read there, *"The Spirit of the Lord is upon me, because he hath anointed me to preach the gospel to the poor"* (Luke 4:18). The poor, then, are among the people intended by the term *the meek.*

I noticed, when I was looking through various comments on this passage, that the Syriac Version renders it "the humble," and I think the Vulgate renders it "the gentle." Calvin translated it "the afflicted." It all comes to one thing: *the meek*—a people who are not lofty in their thoughts, for they have been broken down. They are a people who are not proud and lifted up, but low in their own esteem. They are a people who are often much troubled and tossed about in their thoughts, a people who have lost proud hopes and self-conceited joys. They are a people who seek no high things, crave no honors, desire no praises, but bow before the Lord in humility. They are eager to creep into any hole to hide themselves, because they have such a sense of insignificance and worthlessness and sin. They are a people who are often driven to utter despair.

The meek, the poor—who are meek because they are poor—would be as bold as others if they had as much as others, or as much as others think they have. But God has emptied them, and so they have nothing to boast of. They feel the iniquity of their nature, the plague of their hearts. They mourn that in them there dwells no good thing (Rom. 7:18), and oftentimes they think of themselves as the outcasts of all creation. They imagine themselves to be more brutish than all other men, and quite beneath the Lord's regard. Sin weighs them down, and yet they accuse themselves of insensibility and impenitence.

Now, God has purposely anointed the Lord Jesus to preach the Gospel to such as these. If any of you are good and deserving, the Gospel is not for you. If any of you think that you are keeping God's laws perfectly and hope to be saved by your works, I have to tell you that the whole have no need of a physician (Mark 2:17), and that the Lord Jesus did not come to do so needless an errand as that of healing men who have no wounds or diseases. But the sick need a doctor, and Jesus has come in great compassion to remove their sicknesses.

The more diseased you are, the surer you may be that the Savior came to heal such as you are. The poorer you are, the more certain you may be that Christ came to enrich you. The sadder and more sorrowful you are, the surer you may be that Christ came to comfort you. You nobodies, you who have been turned upside down and emptied right out, you who are bankrupts and beggars, you who feel that you are clothed with rags and covered with wounds and bruises and putrefying sores, you who are utterly bad through and through, and know it and mourn it and are humbled about it, you may know that God has purposely poured the holy oil without measure upon Christ, so that He might deal out mercy to such poor creatures as you are.

What a blessing this is! How we ought to rejoice in the anointing of Jesus, since it benefits such despicable objects! We who feel that we are such objects ought to cry out, *"Hosanna; Blessed is he that cometh in the name of the Lord"* (Mark 11:9).

A Holy Purpose

We must now consider our Lord's purpose and objective in thus preaching the Gospel to the poor and the meek. His purpose, you may observe, was that He might bind up the brokenhearted. *"He hath sent me to bind up the brokenhearted."*

Carefully focus on the meaning of the text, so that you may see whether or not this message applies to you. Are you brokenhearted because of sin, because you have sinned often, foully, grievously? Are you brokenhearted because your heart will not break as you desire it to break—brokenhearted because you are sorry that you cannot repent as you want to and grieved because you cannot grieve enough? Are you brokenhearted because you do not have such a sense of sin as you ought to have and such a deep loathing of it as you perceive others to have?

Are you brokenhearted with despair over trying to save yourself, because you cannot keep God's law, or because you cannot find comfort in ceremonies? Are you brokenhearted because the things that looked best have turned out to be deceptions, or because, all the world over, you have found nothing but broken cisterns, which can hold no water (see Jeremiah 2:13), which have mocked your thirst when you have gone to them? Are you brokenhearted from longing after peace with God, or because prayer does not seem to be answered? Are you brokenhearted because, when you come to hear the Gospel, you fear that it is not applied to you with power, or because you had a little light and yet slipped back into darkness? Are you brokenhearted because you are afraid you have committed the unpardonable sin, or because of blasphemous thoughts that horrify your mind and yet will not leave it? It does not matter for what particular reason you are brokenhearted. Jesus Christ came into the world, sent by God with this purpose: *"to bind up the brokenhearted."*

It is a beautiful idea, this binding up, as though the Crucified One took the liniment and the bandages, put them around the broken heart, and with His own dear, gentle hand proceeded to close up the wound and make it cease to bleed. Luke did not tell us that Jesus came to bind up the brokenhearted; if you examine his version of the text, you will read that He came *to heal them* (Luke 4:18). That is going still further, because you may bind a wound up and yet fail to cure it, but Jesus never fails in His surgery. He whose own heart was broken knows how to cure broken hearts.

I have heard of people dying of a broken heart, but I always bless God when I meet those who live with a broken heart, because it is written, *"A broken and a contrite heart, O God, thou wilt not despise"* (Ps. 51:17). If you have that broken heart within you, beloved, Christ came to cure you; and He will do it, for He never came in vain. *"He shall not fail nor be discouraged"* (Isa. 42:4). With sovereign power, anointed from on high, He watches for the worst of cases. Heart disease, incurable by man, is His specialty! His Gospel touches the root of the soul's illness, the mischief that dwells in that place from which all the issues of life spring (Prov. 4:23).

With pity, wisdom, power, and condescension, He bends over our broken bones; before He has finished with them, He makes them all to rejoice and sing glory to His holy name. Come then, troubled ones, and rely upon your Savior's healing power. Give yourselves up to His care, confide in His skill, and rest in His love. What joy you will have if you will do this at once! What joy I would have in knowing that you did so! Above all, what joy will fill the heart of Jesus, the beloved Physician, as He sees you healed by His stripes!

Chapter 4

The Poor Man's Friend

The poor committeth himself unto thee.
—Psalm 10:14

I want now to refer back to something from our first chapter. In Psalm 22:26, our Lord says, *"The meek shall eat and be satisfied,"* and He is referring to the poor among men, to whom He has always been the source of abounding comfort. We have seen that His Gospel, the Gospel of good tidings, has been preached to the poor and the meek, for Jesus Christ was sent especially to them by the Father. And we have seen how, in Him, the poor may find food for their souls and be satisfied.

Christ is very mindful of the poor and needy. Note what the psalmist wrote about our Lord's protective hand over all who are in need:

He shall deliver the needy when he crieth; the poor also, and him that hath no helper. He shall spare the poor and needy, and shall save the souls of the needy. He shall redeem their soul from deceit and violence: and precious shall their blood be in his sight. (Ps. 72:12–14)

God is the poor man's Friend. The poor man, in his helplessness and despair, leaves his case in the hands of God, and God undertakes to care for him. In the days of David—and I suppose, in this respect, the world has improved very little—the poor man was the victim of almost everybody's cruelty, and at times he was very shamefully oppressed. If he sought redress for the wrongs that had been done to him, he generally only increased them, for he was regarded as a rebel against the existing order of things. And when he asked for even a part of what was his by right, the very magistrates and rulers of the land became the instruments of his oppressors, as they made the yoke of his bondage to be yet heavier than it was before.

Tens of thousands of eyes, full of tears, have been turned to Jehovah, and He has been called upon to intervene between the oppressor and the oppressed, because He is the ultimate resort of the helpless. *"The LORD executeth righteousness and judgment for all that are oppressed"* (Ps. 103:6). He undertakes the cause of all those who are downtrodden.

If the history of the world is interpreted correctly, it will be found that no case of oppression has been allowed to go unpunished for very long. The Syrian empire was a very cruel one, but what is now left of Nineveh and Babylon? Go to the heaps of ruins by the banks of the Tigris and the Euphrates, and see what becomes of an empire that is only an instrument of oppression in the hands of an emperor and the great men under him. The empire is now nothing more than a name; its power has vanished, and its palaces have been destroyed.

In later times, there sprang up the mighty empire of Rome. Even now, wherever we wander, we see traces of its greatness and splendor. How did it fall? Many reasons have been assigned, but you may rest assured that at the bottom of them all was the cruelty practiced toward the slaves and other poor people, who were absolutely in the power of the aristocracy and oligarchy who formed the dominant party in the empire.

There is a fatal flaw in the foundations of any throne that does not execute justice. Although an empire may seem to stand as high as heaven and to raise its pinnacles to the skies, down it must come if it is not founded upon what is right. When ten thousand slaves have cried to God apparently in vain, it has not really been in vain, for He has registered their cries and in due season has avenged their wrongs. And when the poor toilers, who have harvested the rich man's fields and have been deprived of the wages for which they have worked so hard, have cast their complaints into the court of heaven, they have been registered there; at the right time, God has taken up their causes and punished their oppressors.

For many years, the Negro slaves cried to God to deliver them. At last, deliverance came, to the joy of the emancipated multitudes, yet not without suffering to all the nations that had been involved in that great wrong. This principle is something to watch for: if an employer refuses to give his laborers their just wages, God will surely visit him in His wrath.

As I write this, we have workers in England who, with sternest toil, cannot earn enough to keep body and soul together, or to maintain their families as they ought to be maintained. Do the employers, who are thus refusing to give their laborers a fair compensation for their work, not know that God judges the world by this one rule: that men are to do what is just and right to their fellowmen? Some people may excuse them, and they may say that such things can only follow the laws of political economy. But God does not judge the world by political economy. It can never be right that a man should work like a slave, be housed worse than a horse, and have food scarcely fit for a dog. But if the poor commit their case to God, He will undertake it. Personally, as one of God's ministers, I will never cease to speak on behalf of the rights of the poor.

The whole question has two sides: the rights of the employers and the rights of the employees. The laborers should not do as some workers do, asking more than they should. On the other hand, the bosses should not domineer their employees. But let us remember that God is the Master of us all, and He will see that justice is done to all. Let us all act justly toward one another, or we will feel the weight of His hand and the force of His anger.

Now, having thus given the literal meaning of my text, *"The poor committeth himself unto thee,"* I am going to spiritualize it. We will first look closely at the spiritual condition of the men and women whom David called *"the poor,"* and then we will look at what they are moved to do in their poor condition.

The Condition of the Poor

Those who are spiritually poor must do what other poor men have done in regard to temporal things: they must commit their case into the hands of God. But what does it mean to be spiritually poor? What are the characteristics of these people?

Without Personal Merit

The spiritually poor are, first of all, those who have no merits of their own. There are some worldly people who are, according to their own estimate, very rich in good works. They think that they began well and that they have gone on well, and they hope to continue to do well right to the end of their lives. They do confess, sometimes, that they are miserable sinners, but that is merely because that expression is in the church prayer book. They are almost sorry it is there, but they suppose that it must have been meant for other people, not for themselves. As far as they know, they have kept all the commandments from their youth up (Matt. 19:20), they have been just in their dealings with their fellowmen, and they do not feel that they are under any very serious obligations even to God Himself.

I have nothing to say to such people except to remind them that the Lord Jesus Christ said,

> *They that are whole have no need of the physician, but they that are sick: I came not to call the righteous, but sinners to repentance.* (Mark 2:17)

Christ came to bring healing to those who are spiritually sick. If you say that you are perfectly well, then go your own way, and Christ will go in another direction—toward sinners.

Without Strength for Good Works

Further, the poor, of whom I am writing, are not only totally without anything of merit, absolutely bankrupt of any goodness, and devoid of anything of which they could boast, but they are also without strength to perform any such good works in the future. Spiritually, they are so poor that they cannot even pray as they want to, and they do not even feel their poverty as they would like to feel it. After having read the Bible, they wish they could reread it with greater profit.

When they weep over sin, they feel their own sin in their very tears and want to weep even more in penitence because of their tears. They are such poor people that they can do absolutely nothing without Christ; so poor that, in them—that is, in their flesh—there *"dwelleth no good thing"* (Rom. 7:18). They once thought that there might be something good in them, but they have searched their natures thoroughly with great pains, and they have discovered that, unless grace will do everything for them, they can never be where God is.

Perhaps some of you say, "These must be very bad people." Well, they are no worse than many of those who think a great deal better of themselves, and they are certainly not exaggerating their case. They have this lowly opinion of themselves because the grace of God has taught them to think rightly and truthfully about themselves in relation to God. In outward appearance, and as far as we can judge, they are quite as good as others and better than some. In certain respects, they might even be held up as examples to others.

We can say all this about them, but they do not have even one good word to say for themselves. Instead, they put their finger up to their lips and blush at the remembrance of what they feel themselves to be. Or, if they must speak of themselves at all, they say, *"All we like sheep have gone astray; we have turned every one to his own way"* (Isa. 53:6).

What They Do As a Result

That brings me to notice, secondly, what these poor people do as a result of their condition. They commit themselves to God. This is a very blessed description of what true faith does. The poor in spirit feel that their case is so desperate that they cannot keep it in their own charge, and therefore, they commit it to God. I will try to show you how they do that.

The Lord, Their Surety

First, they commit their case to God as a debtor commits his case to a surety, who becomes legally liable for the debt. The man is so deeply in debt that he cannot pay his creditors even a penny on the dollar; but here is someone who can pay everything that the debtor owes. The surety says to the debtor, "I will stand as security for you; I will be a bondsman for you; I will give full satisfaction to all your creditors and discharge all your debts." There is no person who is deeply in debt, who would not be glad to know of such a surety, who is both able and willing to stand in his place and to discharge all his responsibilities. If the surety said to this poor debtor, "Will you give over all your liabilities to me? Will you sign this document, empowering me to take all your debts upon myself and to be responsible for you? Will you let me be your bondsman and surety?" the poor man would reply, "Ah! I will, most gladly."

That is just what spiritually poor men have done to the Lord Jesus Christ—committed their case, with all their debts and liabilities, into His hands—and He has undertaken all the responsibility for them. I can imagine that someone would say, "But will Christ really stand in the sinner's place in such a way as that?" Oh, yes! He did stand in the sinner's place in anticipation, before the foundation of the world. He actually stood there when He died upon the accursed tree, obtaining by His death a full discharge of the debts of all those whose Surety He had become.

Dear soul, will you not commit all your affairs into His hands? Are you not willing to let Him stand as your Surety, to clear you of all your liabilities? "Willing?" you say. "Yes! I am; and I am not only willing, but I will be very glad for Him to take my place and relieve me of the burden that is crushing me to the dust."

Then it is done for you, and so done that it can never be undone.

If you, my dear reader, were to take all my debts upon you, and if you were quite able and willing to pay them, I would not go home and fret about my debts. I would rejoice to think that you had taken them upon yourself and that they would, therefore, no longer be mine. If Christ has taken your sins upon Himself—and He has done so if you have truly trusted Him—then your sins have ceased to be. They are blotted out forever. (See Isaiah 44:22.) Christ nailed to His cross the record of everything that was against us. So now, every poor sinner who is indebted to God's law and who trusts in Christ, may know that his debt is cancelled and that he is clear of all liability for it forever.

The Lord, Their Advocate

Next, the poor and meek commit their case to Christ as a client does to a solicitor and advocate. When a lawsuit is filed against a man, he has an advocate to plead his cause; he does not plead for himself. He will probably get into trouble if he tries to do it himself. It is said that, when Scottish jurist John Erskine was pleading for a man who was being tried for murder, his client, being dissatisfied with the way in which his defense was being conducted, wrote on a slip of paper, "I'll be hanged if I don't plead for myself." Erskine wrote in reply, "You'll be hanged if you do!" It is very much like that with us; if we attempt to plead for ourselves, we will be sure to go wrong. We must have the divine Advocate, who alone can defend us against the suits of Satan and speak with authority on our behalf, even before the bar of God. We must commit our case to Him so that He may plead for us, and then it will go rightly enough.

Remember, also, that any man who has committed his case to an advocate must not interfere with it himself. If anybody from the other side says to him, "I wish to speak to you about that suit," he must reply, "I cannot go into the matter with you; I must refer you to my solicitor." "But I want to reason about it; I want to ask you a few questions about the case." "No," says he, "I cannot listen to what you have to say. You must go to my solicitor." How much trouble Christians would save themselves if, when they have committed their case into the hands of Jesus, they would leave it there, and not attempt to deal with it on their own!

When the Devil comes to tempt me to doubt and fear, I say to him, "I have committed my soul to Jesus Christ, and He will keep it in safety. You must bring your accusations to Him, not to me. I am His client, and He is my Counselor. Why should I have such an Advocate as He is and then plead for myself?" John did not say, "If any man sin, let him be his own advocate"; but he said, *"If any man sin, we have an advocate with the Father, Jesus Christ the righteous"* (1 John 2:1).

Dear brother or sister, leave your case with Christ. He can handle it wisely; you cannot. Remember, if the Devil and you get into an argument, he is much older than you are, far cleverer than you are, and he knows a great many points of law that you do not know. You should always refer him to the Savior, who is older than he is, who knows much more about law and everything else than he does, and who will answer him so effectually as to silence him forever. So, poor, tried, and tempted soul, commit your case to the Great Advocate, and He will plead for you before the King in the court of heaven, and your suit will be sure to succeed through His advocacy.

The Lord, Their Physician

Further, sinners commit their case to Christ as a patient commits his case to a physician. We poor, sin-sick sinners put our souls into the hands of Jesus, so that He may heal us of all our depravities and evil tendencies and infirmities. If anyone asks, "Will He undertake my case if I come to Him?" I answer that He came to be the Physician of souls, and to heal all who trust Him. There never was a case in which He could not heal, for He has a wonderful remedy, a panacea, a cure for all diseases. If you put your case into His hands, the Holy Spirit will shed abroad His love in your heart (Rom. 5:5), and there is no spiritual disease that can withstand that wondrous remedy.

Are you predisposed to quickness of temper? He can cure that. Are you inclined to laziness? Is there a sluggish spirit within you? He can cure that. Are you proud, or are your tendencies toward covetousness, worldliness, lust, or ambition? Christ can cure all these evils. When He was on this earth, He had all kinds of patients brought to Him, yet He never once was baffled by any case. Your case, whatever it may be, will be quite an easy one for Him if you only go and commit it into His hands.

The church often seems to me to be like a great hospital, full of sin-sick souls, and I often pray that the Great Physician will come and heal them. Or, rather, I must correct myself, for He is in the church when His people are gathered to worship Him; He will stay and heal them there. As He walks through the aisles of your church, I urge you to say to Him, "Good Master, I commit myself to You. I take You to be my Savior. Oh, save me from my natural temperament and my besetting sins and everything else that is contrary to Your holy will!" He will hear you, for He never yet has refused to heed the cry of a poor, sin-sick soul. Do not let Him go by you without praying to Him, *"Son of David, have mercy on me"* (Mark 10:47). May the Lord come and lay His hands upon each one of us, and we will be made perfectly whole!

The Lord, Their Captain

As to the future, the spiritually poor commit themselves to Christ in the same way in which the pilgrims described in *The Pilgrim's Progress* commit themselves to the charge of Mr. Greatheart, so that he might fight all their battles for them and conduct them safely to the Celestial City. In the old war times, when the captains of merchant vessels wanted to go to foreign countries and were afraid of being captured by the privateers of other nations, they generally went in a fleet, under the convoy of a man-of-war to protect them. Likewise, that is the way you and I must go to heaven.

Satan's privateers will try to capture us, but we commit ourselves to the protection of Jesus, the Lord High Admiral of all the seas, and we poor little vessels sail safely under His convoy. When any enemy seeks to attack us, we do not need to be afraid. God can blow them all out of the water if He pleases, but He will never allow one of them to injure a solitary vessel that is entrusted to His charge. Sinner, give yourself up to the charge of Jesus, to be convoyed to heaven. You overanxious child of God, lay down all your anxieties at the feet of Jesus, and rest in His infinite power and love, which will never let you be lost.

The Lord, Their Guide

I will use yet another illustration of how the poor commit themselves to Christ. They do it very much in the way in which blind men get themselves to church—by committing themselves to the care of guides. Some blind men can walk a good long way without a guide, but others could not have found their way to church without some friend upon whose arm they could lean.

The way to get to heaven is by leaning upon Jesus. Do not expect to see Him, but trust yourself to Him, and lean hard upon

Him. He loves to be trusted, and faith has a wonderful charm for Him.

I was once near a place called the Mansion House, and as I stood there, a poor blind man, who wished to cross the street to the bank, said to me, "Please, sir, lead me across; I know you will, for I am blind." I was not sure that I could do so, for it is not an easy task to lead a blind man across that intersection, where so many cabs and buses are constantly passing, but I managed it as best I could. I do not think I could have done it if the poor man had not said to me, "I know you will," for then I thought that I must.

If you come to Christ and say, "Lord Jesus, will You lead me to heaven?" and tell Him that you are sure that He will never let a poor, blind soul miss its way, that you are sure you can trust Him, that He is such a kindhearted Savior that He will never thrust away a guilty sinner who thus commits himself into His hands, then I am sure that He will be glad to save you and that He will rejoice over you as He leads you safely home to heaven.

If you can see with your natural eyes and yet are blind spiritually, be glad that there is a blessed Guide to whom you can commit yourself, and do commit yourself to Him. Christ leads the blind by a way that they do not know, and He will continue to lead them until He brings them to the land where they will open their eyes and see with rapture and surprise the splendors of paradise, where they will rejoice that these things are all theirs forever.

Is not this work of the poor committing themselves to Christ a very easy task? It is a very easy thing for a debtor to commit his debt to his surety, for the accused to commit his case to his advocate, for a patient to trust himself to his physician, for a pilgrim to feel safe under a powerful convoy, and for a blind man to trust in his guide—all these are very simple and easy; they do not need much explanation. Well, faith in Jesus is just as simple and easy as that.

Why is it that we sometimes find that faith is difficult? It is because we are too proud to believe in Jesus. If we would only see ourselves as we really are, we would be willing enough to trust the Savior; but we do not like going to heaven as blind people who need a guide, or as debtors who cannot pay a penny on the dollar. We want to have a finger in the pie; we want to do something toward our own salvation; we want to have some of the praise and glory of it. God save us from this evil spirit!

While it is a very simple thing for the spiritually poor to commit themselves to

Christ, let me also say that it is an act that greatly glorifies God. Christ is honored when any soul trusts in Him; it is a joy to His heart to be trusted. When the feeble cling to Him, He feels the kind of joy that mothers feel when their little ones cling to them. Christ is glad when poor, sin-sick souls come and trust Him. It was for this very purpose that He came into the world: to meet the needs of guilty sinners. So this plan, while it is easy for us, is glorifying to Him.

I will also add that it is a plan that never fails any who trust in it. There never was a single soul who committed his case to Christ and then found Him to fail, and there never will be such a soul so long as the earth endures. He who believes in Christ *"shall not be ashamed nor confounded world without end"* (Isa. 45:17). *"He that believeth on the Son hath everlasting life"* (John 3:36), and everlasting life can never be taken away from one who has received it.

At this point, one must ask the question, If the spiritually poor commit themselves to God, what is the result of it? Well, it makes them very happy. But are they not sinful? Oh, yes, but they commit themselves to God's grace, and His grace blots out all their sins forever (Acts 3:19). Are they not feeble? Oh, yes, but their feebleness leads them to commit themselves to His omnipotence, and His strength is made perfect in their weakness (2 Cor. 12:9). Are they not needy? Oh, yes, but then they bring their needs to Him, and they receive out of His fullness *"grace for grace"* (John 1:16). But are they not often in danger? Oh, yes, they are in a thousand dangers, but they come and hide beneath the shadow of God's wings. He covers them with His feathers, and there they rest in perfect security. His truth becomes their shield and buckler, so that they do not need to fear any foe. (See Psalm 91:1–4.)

But are they not apt to slip? Oh, yes, but they commit themselves to Him who gives His angels charge over them, to keep them in all their ways and to bear them up in their hands, lest they should dash their feet against a stone (vv. 11–12). But are they not very fickle and changeable? Oh, yes, but they commit themselves to Him who says, *"I am the LORD, I change not"* (Mal. 3:6). But are they not unworthy? Oh, yes, in themselves they are utterly unworthy, but they commit themselves to Him who is called *"THE LORD OUR RIGHTEOUSNESS"* (Jer. 23:6). When they are clothed in His righteousness, they are looked upon by God as being without *"spot, or wrinkle, or any such thing"* (Eph. 5:27).

But have they no sickness? Yes, but they commit themselves to Jehovah-Rophi, the Lord the Healer, and He either heals their sickness or gives them the grace to endure it. Are they not poor? Yes, many of them are extremely so, but they commit themselves to the faithful Promiser; thus bread is given to them, and they are sure to receive water. But don't they expect to die? Oh, yes, unless the Lord should come before then, but they are not afraid to die. This is the point, above all others, in which the spiritually poor commit themselves unto God. They have learned that sweet prayer of David so well that it is often on their tongues: *"Into thine hand I commit my spirit: thou hast redeemed me, O LORD God of truth"* (Ps. 31:5). They did commit their spirits into God's hand years ago, and He has kept them until now, so they know that He will not fail them in their dying hour.

I pray that every spiritually poor heart would commit himself to God. I like to do this every morning. Satan often comes and says, "You are no Christian; all your supposed Christian experience is false." Very well, suppose it has been false; then I will start afresh. Saint or no saint, I will begin over again by trusting Christ to be my Savior. When you, dear friend, wake tomorrow morning, let this be the first thing that you do—commit yourself to Jesus Christ for the whole of the day. Say, "My Lord, here is my heart, which I commit to You. While I am away from home, may my heart be full of the fragrance of Your blessed presence; when I return at night, may I still find my heart in Your kind keeping!" And every night, before we go to sleep, let us pray,

> Should swift death this night o'ertake us,
> And our couch become our tomb;
> May the morn in heaven awake us,
> Clad in light and deathless bloom.

Are you traveling to a foreign land? Then renew the commitment of your life to God. Are you going to change your state and enter upon the joys and responsibilities of married life? Then commit yourself to God. Are you taking on new employment or opening a new business? Is any change coming over you? Then make a new commitment, or a recommitment, of your soul to the Lord Jesus; only take care that you do it heartily and thoroughly and hold nothing back.

I rejoice to feel that I have committed myself to Christ, just as the slave of old committed himself to his master. When the time came for him to be free under the Jewish law, he said to his master, "No, I do not want to go. I love you, I love your children, I love your household, I love your service; I do not want to be free." Then the master would take an awl and fasten him by the ear to the doorpost. (See Exodus 21:2–6.) I suppose this was done to see whether the man really wanted to remain with his master or not. Ah, dear readers! Some of us have had our ears fastened long ago; we have given ourselves up to Christ, and we have a mark upon us that we can never lose.

Were we not *"buried with him by baptism into death"* (Rom. 6:4)—a symbol that we are dead to the world, and buried to the world—for His dear sake? Well, in that same way, give yourself wholly up to Jesus; commit yourself to Him. As a young bride commits all her life's joys and hopes to the dear bridegroom into whose face she looks so lovingly, so commit yourselves to that dearest Bridegroom in earth or heaven, the Lord Jesus Christ.

Commit yourselves to Him, to love and to be loved—His to obey, His to serve, His to be kept by. Commit to being His in life, and you will not need to add "till death do us part," but you may say, "till death shall wed us more completely, and we shall sit together at the marriage banquet above and be forever and forever one before the throne of God." Thus poor souls commit themselves to Christ, are married to Christ, get the portion that Christ possesses, become Christ's own, and then live with Christ forever.

Oh, that this might be the time in which you, my readers, would commit yourselves to Christ! I do not merely mean you who are poor in purse or pocket, but also you who are poor in spirit. I am asking you to commit yourselves to Christ. Do not put it off, but may this be the very hour in which you will be committed to Christ, and He will take possession of you to be His forever and forever! Amen and Amen.

Chapter 5

Christ Is All

Where there is neither Greek nor Jew,
circumcision nor uncircumcision,
Barbarian, Scythian, bond nor free:
but Christ is all, and in all.
—*Colossians 3:11*

Jesus Christ is our Healer, our Tree of Life. He ministers to the poor and the needy, and He comforts those who are distressed. He is the only One in this entire universe who can keep our souls from the evils of Satan. For these things, and for so much more—in fact, for everything—we are dependent upon Him. He is the Source of everything we will ever need and the One who ties together every loose end in our lives. Indeed, Christ is, as Paul wrote to the Ephesians, our *"all in all"* (Eph. 1:23).

Paul was writing to the Colossians about the new creation, and he said that, in it, *"There is neither Greek nor Jew, circumcision nor uncircumcision, Barbarian, Scythian, bond nor free: but Christ is all."* The new creation is a very different thing from the old one. In the first creation, we are born of the flesh; and that which is born of the flesh is, even at the best, nothing but flesh and can never be anything better. However, in the new creation, we are born of the Spirit, and so we become spiritual and discern spiritual things (1 Cor. 2:14–15). The new life in Christ Jesus is an eternal life, and it links all those who possess it with the eternal realities at the right hand of God above.

In some respects, the new creation is so like the old one that a parallel might be drawn between them. But, in far more respects, it is not at all like the old creation. Many things are absent from the new creation that were found in the old one. Many things that were considered of great value in the first creation are of little or no worth in the new, and many distinctions that were greatly prized in the old creation are treated as mere insignificant trifles in the new creation.

The all-important thing is for each one of us to ask himself or herself the question, Do I know what it is to have been renewed in knowledge after the image of Him who creates anew (Col. 3:10)? Do I know what it is to have experienced the second birth, to have been born again, born from above, by the effectual working of God the Holy Spirit? Do I understand what it is to have spiritually entered a new world *"wherein dwelleth righteousness"* (2 Pet. 3:13)? It is concerning this great truth that I write this particular chapter. First, let us take a close look at what is obliterated when we experience the new birth. After that, we will explore what replaces the old creation.

The Old Creation Erased

First, let us discover what is obliterated when the new creation occurs: *"There is neither Greek nor Jew, circumcision nor uncircumcision, Barbarian, Scythian, bond nor free."*

National Distinctions Are No More

In the kingdom of Christ, there is an obliteration of all national distinctions. I suppose there will always be national distinctions in the world until Christ comes, even if they should all be terminated then. The trouble came about when men tried to build the

Tower of Babel in the plain of Shinar. Their attempts brought babel, or confusion, into the world. The one family of man became transformed into many families—a necessary evil to prevent a still greater one. Unity at Babel would have been far worse than the confusion has ever been.

In the same way, the spiritual unity of Rome, or the papal system, has been infinitely more troublesome to the church and to the world than the division of Christians into various sects and denominations could have ever been. Babel has not been an altogether unmitigated evil; it has, no doubt, brought about a certain amount of good and prevented colossal streams of evil from reaching a still more awful culmination. Still, the separation is, in itself, an evil; and it is, therefore, in the Lord's own time and way, to be done away with. Spiritually, it is already abolished.

In the church of Christ, wherever there is real unity of heart among believers, nationality is no hindrance to true Christian fellowship. I feel just as much love toward any brother or sister in Christ who is not of my race as I do toward our own Christian countrymen and countrywomen. Indeed, I sometimes think I feel the force of the spiritual union even more when I catch the Swiss accent or the French or the German, breaking out in the midst of the English, as I often do in my own church, thank God. I seem to feel all the more interest in these beloved brothers and sisters because of the small difference in nationality that there is between us. Certainly, dear believers, in any part of the true church of Christ, all national distinctions are swept away, and we *"are no more strangers and foreigners, but fellowcitizens with the saints, and of the household of God"* (Eph. 2:19).

Under the Christian dispensation, the distinction or division of nationality has gone from us in this sense. We once had our national heroes—in fact, each nation still glories in its great men of the heroic age or in its mythical heroes—but the one Champion and Hero of Christianity is our Lord Jesus Christ, who has slain our dragon foes, routed all our adversaries, broken down the massive fortress of our great Enemy, and set the captives free. We no longer sing of the valiant deeds of national heroes—Saint George, Saint Andrew, Saint Patrick, Saint Denis, and the other so-called saints, who were either only legendary or else anything but "saints," as we understand the term. We sing the prowess of the King of all saints, the mighty Son of David, who is worthy of our loftiest singing.

We are quite willing to forget King Arthur and the knights of the Round Table, when we think of *"another king, one Jesus"* (Acts 17:7), and of another table, where they who sit are not merely good knights of Jesus Christ, but are made kings and priests unto Him (Rev. 1:6) who sits at the head of the festal table. Barbarian, Scythian, Greek, Jew—these distinctions are all gone as far as we are concerned, for we are all one in Christ Jesus. We do not boast of our national or natural descent, or of the heroes whose blood may be in our veins. It is enough for us that Christ has lived, Christ has died, and Christ has *"spoiled principalities and powers"* (Col. 2:15) and trampled down sin, death, and hell, even as He fell amid the agonies of Calvary.

Away, too, has gone all our national history, so far as there may have been any desire to exalt it for the purpose of angering Christian brothers and sisters of another race. I wish that even the names of wars and famous battlefields could be altogether forgotten. But, if they do remain in the memories of those of us who are Christians, we will not boast as he did who said, "But 'twas a famous victory," nor will we proudly sing of

> The flag that braved a thousand years
> The battle and the breeze.

As Christians, our true history has no beginning except in that dateless eternity when the Holy Trinity in unity conceived the wondrous plan of predestinating grace, electing love, the substitutionary sacrifice of the Son of God for the sins of His chosen people, the full and free justification of all who believe, and the eternal glory of the whole redeemed family of God. This is our past, present, and future history. We who are Christians take down the Book in which these things are written, and we make our boast in the Lord, and thus the boasting is not sinful.

As to laws and customs, of which each nation has its own, it is not wrong for a Christian to take delight in a good custom that has been long established, nor is it wrong for him to fight to maintain ancient laws, which have preserved as sacred the liberty of the people for ages upon ages. But, still, the customs of Christians are learned from the example of Christ, and the laws of believers are the precepts laid down by Him. When we are dealing with matters relating to the church of Christ, we have no English customs, no French customs, no American customs, no German customs. If we do have them, we should let them go and have only Christian customs from now on.

Did our Lord Jesus Christ command anything? Then let it be done. Did He forbid anything? Then do away with it. Would He smile upon a certain action? Then perform it at once. Would He frown upon it? Then watch that you do the same. Blessed is the believer who has realized that the laws and customs to be observed by the people of God are plainly written out in the life of Christ and that He has now become to us, *"all, and in all."*

Christ, by giving liberty to all His people, has obliterated the distinctions of nationality that we once attributed to various countries. One remembers, with interest, the old declaration, *"Romanus sum"* ("I am a Roman"), because a citizen of Rome, wherever he might have been, felt that he was a free man whom no one would dare to hurt, or else Roman legions would ask the reason why. Likewise, an Englishman, in every country, wherever he may be, still feels that he is one who was born free and who would sooner die than become a slave or hold another man or woman in slavery. But, brothers and sisters, there is a higher liberty than this, and that is the liberty with which Christ has made His people free.

When we come into the church of God, we talk about that liberty. We believe that Christians, even if they do not have the civil and religious rights that we possess, are still as free in Christ as we are. There are still many, in various parts of the world, who do not enjoy the civil liberties that we have, but who, notwithstanding their bonds, are spiritually free; for, as the Son has made them free, they are free indeed (John 8:36).

Christ also takes from us all inclination or power to boast of our national prestige. To me, it is prestige enough to be a Christian—to bear the cross Christ gives me to carry and to follow in the footsteps of the great Crossbearer. What is the power, in which some boast, in sending soldiers and weapons to a distant shore compared with the almighty power with which Christ guards the weakest of us who dares to trust Him? What reason is there for a man to be puffed up with pride just because he happens to have been born in this or that highly favored country? What is such a privilege compared with the glories that belong to the man who is born again from above, who is an heir of heaven, who is a child of God through faith in Jesus Christ, and who can truthfully say, "All things are mine, and I am Christ's, and Christ is God's"? (See 1 Corinthians 3:21, 23.)

What is this wondrous internationalism that equalizes all these various nationalities in the church of Christ and makes us all one in

Him? Spiritually, we have all been born in one country; the New Jerusalem is the mother of us all. It is not my boast that I am a citizen of this or that earthly city or town. Instead, it is my joy that I am one of the citizens of *"a city which hath foundations, whose builder and maker is God"* (Heb. 11:10). Christ has fired all of us who are His people with a common enthusiasm. He has revealed Himself to each one of us as He does not unto the world. In the happy remembrance that we belong to Him, we forget that we are called by this or that national name and only remember that He is our Lord and that we are to follow where He leads the way.

He has pointed us to heaven, as the leader of the Goths and Huns pointed his followers to Italy and said, "There is the country whence come the luscious wines of which you have tasted. Go, take the vineyards, and grow the vines for yourselves." Those people forgot that they belonged to various tribes, and they all united under the one commander who promised to lead them on to the conquest of the rich land for which they yearned. And now, we who are in Christ Jesus, having tasted of the Eshcol clusters (see Numbers 13:24) that grow in the heavenly Canaan, follow our glorious Leader and Commander as the Israelites followed

Joshua. We forget that we belong to so many different tribes, knowing that there is an inheritance reserved in heaven for all who follow where Jehovah-Jesus leads the way.

Ceremonial Distinctions Are No More

The next thing to be observed in our text is that ceremonial distinctions are obliterated. When Paul said that *"there is neither circumcision nor uncircumcision,"* he recalled the fact that, under the Law, there were some who were specially considered the children of promise, to whom were committed the oracles of God (Rom. 3:2). But there is no such thing as that now. Then there were others, who stood outside the limits of the Law—the sinners of the Gentiles, who were left in darkness until their time for receiving the light should come. But Christ has fused these two into one; and, now, in His church, *"there is neither Greek nor Jew."*

I marvel at the insanity of those who try to prove that we are Jews—the lost ten tribes, indeed! I admit that the business transactions of a great many citizens of London provide some support for the theory, but it is only a theory, and a very crazy one, too. But suppose they were able to prove that we are of the seed of Abraham, after the flesh. It would not make any difference to us, for we are expressly told that *"there is neither Greek nor Jew, circumcision nor uncircumcision,"* for all believers are one in Christ Jesus. The all-important consideration is, Are we Christians? Do we really believe in Jesus Christ to the salvation of our souls?

The apostle rightly said, *"Christ is all,"* for He has done away with all the distinctions that formerly existed between Jews and Gentiles. He has leveled down, and He has leveled up. First, He has leveled down the Jews and made them stand in the same class as the Gentiles, shutting them up under the custody of the very Law in which they gloried and making them see that they can never come out of that bondage except by using the key of faith in Christ.

On the other hand, He has leveled up the outcast and despised Gentiles, having admitted us to all the privileges of His ancient covenant. He has made us to be heirs of Abraham in a spiritual sense, *"though Abraham be ignorant of us, and Israel acknowledge us not"* (Isa. 63:16). To us He has given all the blessings that belong to Abraham's seed, because we, too, possess a faith as precious as the "father of the faithful" himself had. So, our Lord Jesus has stopped the mouths of both Jews and Gentiles and has made them stand equally guilty before God.

That is why we can say,

> *Now in Christ Jesus* [we] *who sometimes were far off are made nigh by the blood of Christ. For he is our peace, who hath made both one, and hath broken down the middle wall of partition between us; having abolished in his flesh the enmity, even the law of commandments contained in ordinances; for to make in himself of twain one new man, so making peace.* *(Eph. 2:13–15)*

Oh, what a blessing it is that all national and ceremonial distinctions are gone forever and that *"Christ is all"* to all who believe in Him!

Social Distinctions Are No More

A more difficult point, perhaps, is that of social distinctions, but that also has been erased from the church of Christ. *"There is neither bond nor free,"* said the apostle. Well, blessed be God, slavery has almost ceased to exist. Among Christians it has become a byword, a passing phrase, though there was a time when some of them pleaded for it as a divinely ordained institution. But, oh, may the last vestige of it speedily disappear, and may every man see it to be both his duty and his privilege to yield to his fellowman his God-given rights and liberties!

Yet, even in a free country such as England, there are still distinctions between classes, and I expect there always will be. I do not suppose there ever can be any system in this world in which everybody will be equal, even if we could have the profoundest philosophers to invent it. Or, if they ever should be all equal, they would not remain so for more than five minutes. We are not all equal in our form or shape or capacity or ability, and we never will be.

Think of your own body. You could not have the various parts of your body all equal; if you had such an arrangement as that, your body would be a monstrosity. There are some parts of the body that must have a more honorable office and function than others have, but all the members are in the body and necessary to its proper symmetry and harmony. So it is in the church of Christ, which is His spiritual body.

Yet, dear friends, how very, very minute are the distinctions between the various members of that body! Perhaps you are rich, as the world reckons riches. Well, do not boast of your wealth, for riches are very likely to take wings and fly away. Most likely, more of you are poor, as far as worldly wealth is concerned. Well, then, do not murmur, for *"all things are yours"* (1 Cor. 3:21) if you are Christ's. Soon, you will be where you will know nothing of poverty again forever and ever.

True Christianity wipes out all these distinctions in a practical way by saying, "This man, as one of Christ's stewards, has more of his Lord's money entrusted to him than others have, so he is bound to do more with it than they do with their portion; he must give away more then they do." One man apparently has far less than his rich brother, but Christ says that he is responsible for the proper use of what he has and not for what he does not have. As the poor widow's two mites drop into the treasury of the Lord, He receives her gift with as sweet a smile as that which He granted to the lavish gifts of David and Solomon. In His church, Christ teaches us that if we have more than others, we simply hold it in trust for those who have less than we have.

And I believe that some of the Lord's children are poor in order that there may be an opportunity for their fellow Christians to minister to them out of their abundance. We could not prove our devotion to Christ in the kind of practical service that He loves best, if there were not needy ones whom we could relieve and support. Our Lord has told us how He will say, in the great Day of Reckoning, *"I was an hungered, and ye gave me meat"* (Matt. 25:35); but that could not be the case if none of *"the least of...*[His] *brethren"* (v. 40) were hungry and if there were none whom we could feed for His sake. *"I was thirsty, and ye gave me drink"* (v. 35), He will say. But He could not say that if none of His poor children were thirsty. *"I was sick, and ye visited me"* (v. 36). So, there must be sick saints to be visited and cases of distress of various kinds to be relieved; otherwise, there could not be the opportunity of practically proving our love to our Lord.

In the church of Christ, it should always be so. We should *"love one another with a pure heart fervently"* (1 Pet. 1:22); we should bear each other's burdens *"and so fulfil the law of Christ"* (Gal. 6:2); and we should care for one another (1 Cor. 12:25). As far as we can, we should seek to supply one another's needs. The rich brother must not exalt himself above the poor one, nor must the poor Christian envy his richer brothers and sisters in Christ. In Him, all these distinctions are obliterated, and we sit down at His table as members of the one family of which He is the glorious and ever living Head. And we *"dwell together in unity"* (Ps. 133:1), praising Him that national, ceremonial, and social distinctions have all passed away for us and that *"Christ is all, and in all."*

The New Creation Replaces the Old

Now that I have described what is obliterated from the old creation, I will try to show you what takes its place in the new creation: *"Christ is all, and in all."*

Christ, Our Culture

First, Christ is all our culture. Has Christianity wiped out that grand name *Greek?* Yes, in the old meaning of it; and in some ways it is a great pity that it is gone, for the Greek was a cultured man. The Greek's every movement was elegance itself, and the Greek was the standard of classic beauty and eloquence. But Christianity has wiped all that out and written in its place, *"Christ is all."* The culture, the gracefulness, the beauty, the comeliness, the eloquence—in the sight of the best Judge of all those things, namely, God, the Ever Blessed—that Christ gives to the true Christian, are better than all that Greek art or civilization ever produced. So we may cheerfully let it all go, and say, *"Christ is all."*

Christ, Our Revelation

Next, Christ is all our revelation. The Jews were fine fellows, and there is still much to admire in them. The Semitic race seems to have been specially constituted by God for devout worship. The Jew, the descendant of believing Abraham, is still a firm believer in one part of God's Word. The Jew is, spiritually, a staunch conservative in that matter, the very backbone of the world's belief. What a pity that his faith is so incomplete and that there is mingled with it so much tradition received from his fathers! Will you wipe out that name *Jew?* Yes, because we who believe in Jesus glory in Him even as the Jew gloried in having received the oracles of God. Christ is the incarnate Word of God, and all the divine revelation is centered in Him. We hold fast the eternal verities that have been committed unto us, because of the power of Christ that rests upon us.

Christ, Our Ritual

Then, next, Christ is all our ritual. There is no mandatory circumcision for spiritual membership in the body of Christ now. That is the special mark of those who are separated from all the rest of mankind; they bear in their bodies the undisputed indications that they are set apart to be the Lord's special possession. Someone asks, "Will you do away with that distinguishing rite?" Yes, we will; for in Christ every true Christian is set apart unto God, marked as Jesus Christ's special, separated one by the circumcision made without hands (Col. 2:11). Now, true *"circumcision is that of the heart, in the spirit, and not in the letter"* (Rom. 2:29).

Christ, Our Simplicity

Further, Christ is all our simplicity. Suppose a man says, "Uncircumcision is my distinguishing mark," to which he adds, "I am not separated or set apart from others as the so-called 'priest' is; I am a man among my fellowmen. Wherever I go, I can mingle with others and feel that they are my brothers. I belong to the 'uncircumcision.' Will you rule that out also?" Yes, we will, because we have in Christ all that uncircumcision means. He who becomes a real Christian is the truest of all men; he is the freest from that spirit that says, *"Stand by thyself, come not near to me;*

for I am holier than thou" (Isa. 65:5). He is the true philanthropist, the real lover of men, even as Christ was.

Christ was no separatist in the sense in which some use that word. He went to a wedding feast; He ate bread in the house of a publican; and a woman of the city, who was a sinner, was permitted to wash His feet with her tears. He mingled with the rest of mankind, and *"the common people heard him gladly"* (Mark 12:37). He would have us to be as He was, the true Man among men, the great Lover of mankind.

Christ, Our Tradition

Once more, Christ is all our natural traditions, our unconquerableness and liberty. I can imagine a rude barbarian saying, "I will never give up the free, manly life that I have lived so long. By my unshorn beard"—for that is the meaning of the term *barbarian*—"I swear it will be so." The nomadic Scythian, likewise, says, "By the wild steppes and wide plains, over which I roam unconquerable, I will never bend to the conventionalities of civilization and be the slave of your modern luxuries."

Well, it is almost a pity to have no further concern with barbarians and Scythians, in this sense, for there is a good deal about them to be commended; but we must wipe them all out. If they come into the church, Christ must be *"all, and in all,"* because everything that is manly, everything that is natural, everything that is free, everything that is bold, everything that is unconquerable will be put into them if *"Christ is all"* to them. They will receive all the qualities that are in that freedom, without the faults belonging to it.

Christ, Our Master

Further, *"Christ is all"* as our Master, if we are *"bond,"* meaning, if we are slaves. I can imagine, in the great assembly at Colossae, which Paul addressed, one who said, "But I am a bondservant. A man bought me at the auction, and here on my back are the marks of the slaveholder's lash." And he must have added, "I wish that this disgrace could be wiped out." But Paul said, "Brother, it *is* wiped out. You are no bondservant, really, for Christ has made you free." Then the great Apostle to the Gentiles came and sat down by his side, and said to him, "The church of Christ has absorbed you, brother, by making us all like you, for we are all servants of one Master." As Paul bared his own back and showed the scars from his repeated scourgings, he said, *"Henceforth let no man trouble me: for I bear in my body the marks of the Lord Jesus"* (Gal. 6:17). Laying his hand on the poor Christian slave, he said, "I, Paul, the slave of Jesus Christ, share your servitude, and with me you are Christ's freeman."

Christ, Our Freedom

Lastly, Christ is our Magna Carta; He is our liberty itself if we are *"free."* Along comes the freeman, who was born free. Can that clause stand, *"neither bond nor free"?* Oh, yes, let it stand, but not so that we glory in our national freedom, for Christ has given us a higher freedom. I may slightly alter the familiar couplet and say

He is the free man whom THE LORD makes free,
And all are slaves beside.

Oh, what multitudes of people are slaves—miserable slaves to the opinions of their neighbors, slaves to the caprices of the prudish, slaves to "respectability"! Some of you dare not do a thing that you know to be right because somebody might make a remark about it. What are you but slaves? Every Sunday there are slaves in the pulpit who dare not speak the truth for fear that somebody will be offended. There are also slaves in the pews and slaves in the shops and slaves all around. What a wretched life a slave lives! Yet, until you become a Christian and know what it is to wear Christ's bonds about your willing wrists, you will always feel the galling, irritating fetters of society and the bonds of custom, fashion, or this or that. But Jesus makes us free with a higher freedom, so we wipe out the mere terrestrial freedom that is too often only a sham, and we write, *"Christ is all."*

So, to conclude, remember this: if you have Christ as your Savior, you do not need anybody else to save you. There is an old gentleman in Rome with a triple crown on his head. We do not need him, for *"Christ is all."* He says that he is God's appointed representative on earth. That is not true; but if it were, it would not matter, for *"Christ is all,"* so we can do without the Pope. Another gentleman tells me that he can give me absolution if I will confess my sins to him as the priest of the parish. But, seeing that *"Christ is all,"* we can do without that gentleman as well as the other one, for anything that is over and above *"all"* must be superfluous, if not worse.

So it is with everything that is beside or beyond Christ. Faith can get to Christ without

Pope or priest. Everything that is outside Christ is a lie, for *"Christ is all."* All that is true must be inside Him, so we can do without all others in the matter of our souls' salvation.

But, supposing that we have not received Christ as our Savior, then how unspeakably poor we are! If we have not grasped Christ by faith, we have not laid hold of anything, for *"Christ is all."* If we do not have Him who is all, then we have nothing at all. "Oh!" says one, "I am a regular churchgoer." Yes, so far, so good; but if you do not have Christ, you have nothing, for *"Christ is all."* "But I have been baptized," says another. Ah! But if you have not trusted in Christ for salvation, your baptism is only another sin added to all your others. "But I go to communion," says another. So much the worse for you if you have not trusted in Christ as your Savior.

I wish I could put this thought into the heart of everyone reading this who is without Christ. Better still, I pray the Holy Spirit to impress this thought upon your heart: if you are without Christ, you are without everything that is worth having, for *"Christ is all."*

But, Christians, I would like to make your hearts dance by reminding you that, if you have Christ as your Savior, you are rich in the full meaning of bliss, for you have *"all"* that your heart can wish to have. Nobody else can say as much as that, for even the richest man in the world has only gotten "something," though the something may be very great. Alexander conquered one world; but you, believer, in receiving Christ as your own, have this world and also that which is to come, life and death, time and eternity. Oh, revel in the thought that, as Christ is yours, you are rich to an infinite degree of riches, for *"Christ is all."*

Now, if Christ really is yours, and as Christ is *"all,"* then love Him, honor Him, and praise Him. Mother, what were you doing this afternoon? Were you holding that dear child of yours close to you and saying, "She is my all"? Take back those words, for they are not true. If you love Christ, He is your *"all,"* and you cannot have another "all." Someone else has one who is very near and very dear. If you are that someone else, and you have said in your heart, "He is my all," or, "She is my all," you have done wrong, for nothing and no one but Christ must be your *"all."* You will be an idolater, and you will grieve the Holy Spirit, if anything or anyone except Christ becomes your *"all."*

You who have lately lost your loved ones and you who have been brought low by recent losses in business, are you fretting over your losses? If so, remember that you have not lost your *"all."* You still have Christ, and He is *"all."* Then, what have you lost? Yes, I know that you have something to grieve over; but, after all, your *"light affliction, which is but for a moment, worketh for* [you] *a far more exceeding and eternal weight of glory"* (2 Cor. 4:17). Therefore, comfort yourself with this thought: "I have not really lost anything, for I still have all." When you have all things, find Christ in all; and when you have lost all things, then find all things in Christ. I do not know for sure, but I think that the latter is the better of the two.

Now, if *"Christ is all,"* then, beloved brothers and sisters, let us live for Him. If He is all, let us spend our strength; let us be ready to lay down the last particle of it that we have and to die for Him. And then let us, whenever we need anything, go to Him for it, for *"Christ is all."* Let us draw upon this bank, for its resources are infinite; we will never exhaust them.

Lastly and chiefly, let us send our hearts right on to where He is. Where our treasure is, there should our hearts be also (Matt. 6:21). Come, my heart, up and away! What do you have here that can fill you? What do you have here that can satisfy you? Plume your wings, and be up and away, for there is your roosting place. There is the Tree of Life that can never be felled. Up and away, and build there forever! The Lord help each one of you to do so, for Jesus' sake! Amen.

Chapter 6

Marvelous Lovingkindness

Show thy marvellous lovingkindness.
—Psalm 17:7

The Lord's people, in the time of their trouble, know where to go for comfort and relief. Being taught by God, they do not hew out for themselves broken cisterns, which can hold no water (Jer. 2:13). Instead, they turn to the ever flowing Fountain, they go to the Source of the well, even to God Himself, where they cast themselves down and drink to the full. David, when he wrote Psalm 17, was evidently in very great distress; therefore, he said, *"I have called upon thee, for thou wilt hear me, O God: incline thine ear unto me, and hear my speech"* (v. 6). What he wanted was his God. Dr. Isaac Watts, an English hymnwriter, expressed it this way:

In darkest shades if he appear,
My dawning is begun;
He is my soul's sweet morning star,
And he my rising sun.

Believers draw comfort from both God's ordinary and extraordinary dealings with them, for they regard God's lovingkindness as being both an ordinary and an extraordinary thing. I have heard of a good sister in Christ who, when a friend narrated to her some very gracious act of God, was asked the question, "Is it not very wonderful?" She replied, "No, it is not wonderful, for it is just like Him." Begging her pardon and admitting the great truth that she meant to convey, I think it is still more wonderful that it is "just like Him." The wonder of extraordinary love is that God has made it such an ordinary thing. He has given to us "*marvellous lovingkindness,*" and He gives it so often that it becomes a daily blessing and yet remains marvelous still.

The marvels of men, after you have seen them a few times, cease to excite any wonder. I suppose there is scarcely a building, however costly its material and however rare its architecture, about which you will not sooner or later feel that you have seen enough of it. But God's wonderful works never lose their interest for you. You could gaze upon Mont Blanc, or you could stand and watch Niagara Falls, yet you would never feel that you had exhausted all its marvels. And everyone knows how the ocean is never the same twice. Those who live close to it and look upon it every hour of the day still see God's wonders in the deep.

That God blesses us every day is a subject for our comfort. God's ordinary ways charm us. The verse before our text says, *"I have called upon thee, for thou wilt hear me, O God"* (Ps. 17:6). I can imagine that David continued, "I know You will, for the blessing that I am about to ask from You is a thing that I have been accustomed to receiving from You. I know You will hear me, for You have heard me in the past; it is a habit of Yours to listen to my supplications and to grant my requests." I hope we can present our case before God in a similar fashion.

Yet, at the same time, God's people draw equal comfort from the extraordinary character of the mercies He bestows upon them. They appeal to Him to show them His *"marvellous lovingkindness,"* to let them see the wonderful side of it as well as the common side of it, to let them behold His miracles of mercy, His extravagances of love, His excesses of kindness. I scarcely know what words to use when writing of what the apostle Paul called *"the riches of his grace; wherein he hath abounded toward us in all wisdom and prudence"* (Eph. 1:7), and *"the exceeding riches of his grace in his kindness toward us through Christ Jesus"* (Eph. 2:7).

I want, at this time, to dwell upon the extraordinary side of God's lovingkindness. Using our text as a prayer, I also want to say to the Lord in the language of David, *"Show thy marvellous lovingkindness."* Sometimes a man is brought into such a condition that he feels that he will surely perish if God does not do something quite out of the ordinary. He has come to such odds that he will be ruined if some extraordinary grace is not displayed toward him. Well, now, such a brother may think that God will not give this extraordinary grace to him. He may be troubled at the idea that some marvelous thing is needed from God. It is in response to that suggestion of unbelief that I write the following words.

His Lovingkindness Is Marvelous

My first remark is that all the lovingkindness of God is marvelous. The least mercy from God is a miracle. That God does not crush our sinful race is a surprising mercy. That you and I have been spared to live—even if we live in direst poverty or in sorest sickness—that we should have been spared at all, after what we have been and after what we have done, is a very marvelous thing. The explanation of the marvel is given in the book of Malachi: *"I am the LORD, I change not; therefore ye sons of Jacob are not consumed"* (Mal. 3:6).

If God possessed a short temper such as men often have, He would have made short work of us all. However, He is gracious and longsuffering, and, therefore, He is very patient with us. The very least mercy that we ever receive from God is a very wonderful thing. Yet, when we think of all that is meant by this blessed word *lovingkindness*—which is a compound of all sorts of sweetnesses, a mixture of fragrances to make up one absolutely perfect perfume—when we take that word *lovingkindness* and ponder over its meaning, we will see that what it describes is indeed a marvelous thing.

It Is Eternal

His lovingkindness is marvelous for its antiquity. To think that God should have had lovingkindness toward men *"from the beginning, or ever the earth was"* (Prov. 8:23); to think that there should have been a covenant of election, a plan of redemption, a scheme of atonement; to think that there should have been eternal thoughts of love in the mind of God toward such a strange being as man—these thoughts are indeed marvelous. *"What is man, that thou art mindful of him? and the son of man, that thou visitest him?"* (Ps. 8:4). Read these words with tears in your eyes: *"I have loved thee with an everlasting love: therefore with lovingkindness have I drawn thee"* (Jer. 31:3); and when you know that this passage refers to you, tell me if it is not *"marvellous lovingkindness."*

God's mind is occupied with thoughts concerning things that are infinitely greater than the destiny of any one of us, or of all of us put together. Even so, He was pleased to think of us in love from all eternity and to write our names upon His hands (see Isaiah 49:16) and upon His heart, and to keep the remembrance of us perpetually before Him, for His *"delights were with the sons of men"* (Prov. 8:31). This antiquity makes it to be, indeed, *"marvellous lovingkindness."*

It Is Discriminating

Next, God's lovingkindness is marvelous for its discriminating, or distinguishing, character.

The poorest, the most illiterate, the most obscure, and often the guiltiest of our race are the recipients of His lovingkindness. Remember what Paul wrote about this matter:

> *Not many wise men after the flesh, not many mighty, not many noble, are called: but God hath chosen the foolish things of the world to confound the wise; and God hath chosen the weak things of the world to confound the things which are mighty; and base things of the world, and things which are despised, hath God chosen, yea, and things which are not, to bring to nought things that are: that no flesh should glory in his presence.* (1 Cor. 1:26–29)

Dr. Watts expressed the same thought in these verses:

> When the Eternal bows the skies
> To visit earthly things,
> With scorn divine he turns his eyes
> From towers of haughty kings.
>
> He bids his awful chariot roll
> Far downward from the skies,
> To visit every humble soul,
> With pleasure in his eyes.

God's choice is marvelous. I know of no better word to apply to His lovingkindness to His chosen ones than that which is applied in the text: *"thy marvellous lovingkindness."*

What was there in you that could merit esteem,
 Or give the Creator delight?
"'Twas even so, Father," you ever must sing,
 "Because it seem'd good in thy sight."

There is no other explanation for this wondrous mercy, this *"marvellous lovingkindness,"* than the poet gave:

His love, from eternity fix'd upon you,
 Broke forth, and discover'd its flame,
When each with the cords of his kindness he drew,
 And brought you to love his great name.

So, beloved child of God, think of the antiquity of God's lovingkindness and then of the discriminating character of it, and surely you will be full of adoring wonder.

It Is Self-sacrificing

After that, His lovingkindness is marvelous for its self-sacrificing nature. God had set His heart on man and had chosen His people before the foundation of the world, so that He could then give—what? Himself. Yes, Himself and nothing short of that. Think how He not only gives us this world and His providence and all its blessings and the world to come and all its glories, but, in order to ensure our possession of these things, He gave His own Son to die for us.

The apostle John did well to write, *"Herein is love, not that we loved God, but that he loved us, and sent his Son to be the propitiation for our sins"* (1 John 4:10). It was not that Christ died for us when we were righteous, *"for scarcely for a righteous man will one die...but God commendeth his love toward us, in that, while we were yet sinners, Christ died for us"* (Rom. 5:7–8). *"When we were yet without strength, in due time Christ died for the ungodly"* (v. 6). Isaiah had long before explained the mystery: *"It pleased the LORD to bruise him; he hath put him to grief"* (Isa. 53:10).

You who love your children so much that to lose one of them would be worse than to die, can realize a little of what must have been the Father's love for you in giving up His only begotten Son so that you might live through Him. Dwell on this great truth, dear friends, meditate on it, and ask the Holy Spirit to lead you into its heights and depths, its lengths and breadths, for I cannot fully tell of its wonders. As you think over the Lord's ancient lovingkindnesses, which always existed, His distinguishing love toward His redeemed, and His self-sacrificing love in giving up His Only Begotten, you will be obliged to say, "It is marvelous lovingkindness; it is marvelous lovingkindness, indeed."

It Is Constant

Then, His lovingkindness is marvelous for the constancy of it. It is not so very amazing that one begins to love another, but it is wonderful when the love, after it has been despised and unrequited, still continues. It is an extraordinary thing, that the sweet love of Christ did not long ago curdle into jealousy, and, from jealousy, sour into indignation. He loved us, brothers and sisters, when we did not even know Him, and yet we hated the Unknown. He loved us when we did not even dimly understand His love for us and perhaps even ridiculed it, or at least neglected it. He kept on loving us until He loved us into loving Him.

But even since then, what has our character been? Are you satisfied with how you have acted toward the Well Beloved? Are you content with your conduct toward the Bridegroom of your souls? I think that you are not. Yet, notwithstanding your lukewarmness, your backsliding, your dishonoring of His name, your unbelief, your pride, your love of others, He still loves you. Even now, if you are not enjoying fellowship with Him, He has not gone away from you, for His word still is, *"Behold, I stand at the door, and knock"* (Rev. 3:20). He loves, He loves on, and He loves still. *"Many waters cannot quench* [His] *love, neither can the floods drown it"* (Song 8:7). It is indeed *"marvellous lovingkindness."*

Can you think of a better adjective than that? I cannot, yet I am conscious that even that does not fully express the miraculous character of this all-enduring love that will not take our no for an answer but still says, "Yes, *'I will betroth thee unto me in righteousness, and in judgment, and in lovingkindness, and in mercies. I will even betroth thee unto me in faithfulness: and thou shalt know the LORD'* (Hos. 2:19)." Oh, this wonderful, this matchless, this unparalleled, this inconceivable, this infinite love! No human language can adequately describe it, so let us sit still and marvel at that which we cannot even understand.

It Is Creative

God's lovingkindness is marvelous in its strange ingenuity. I might write on this topic forever, applying one word and another to it;

but I still will not have shown you even a tenth of its wonders, for it is an altogether inexhaustible subject. It is wonderful how God deals with us with such a sacred yet creative tenderness. He seems to be always thinking of something for our good, while we, on our part, appear to be always testing His love in one way or another. As soon as a fresh need is discovered, we receive a new supply of grace. If a fresh sin breaks out, it is blotted out with the ever pardoning blood of Jesus. We get into fresh difficulties only to receive fresh aid.

The further I go on my way to heaven, the more I admire the road as well as wonder at the goal to which that road will bring me. "O world of wonders!" said John Bunyan. "I can say no less." They tell us, nowadays, that the world is worn out, that there is no joy in life, and that there is nothing fresh to give us delight. Ah, me! They talk of the attractions of fiction and of the playwright's art, and I do not know what else. They need to travel all around the world to get a new sensation. Many a man today is like the Emperor Tiberius, who offered large sums of money to anyone who could invent a new pleasure, which, unfortunately, too often means a new vice or a new way of practicing it.

But staying at home with Christ has more wonders in it than wandering abroad with all the wisest of the world. There is more to marvel at in half an inch of the way to heaven than there is in a thousand leagues of the ordinary pathway of unbelieving men. They call their joys by the name of "life" and say that they must "see life"; but the apostle John told us that *"he that hath the Son hath life; and he that hath not the Son of God hath not life"* (1 John 5:12).

Obviously, one who does not have life is dead. Death has its varieties of worms and rottenness; there are charnel houses and more charnel houses, various processes and methods of corruption, and no doubt there is a science that men may learn in the cemetery and call it life, if they like. Oh! But if they could only see Christ upon the cross for one moment, they would learn that they had been blind until then. If they could only know His lovingkindness, they would rejoice in it in the sickroom, in the long weary night watches, when every bone prevents sleep. They would even recognize it in the arrows of death that strike and kill their wives and their children and their brothers and sisters.

They would see His lovingkindness not only in the table loaded for the relief of hunger and in the garments furnished against the cold and in every common blessing of providence; but they would also see it in every despondency, in every deficiency, in every cross, and in every loss. Then, seeing it, they would keep on saying, "It is all for the best; it is all better than the best could have been if it had been left to me. It is marvelous; it is marvelous lovingkindness." I do believe that when we get to heaven, one of the wonders of the glory land will be to look back upon the road over which we have traveled. It will be marvelous to note the way in which God has led us. As the hymn puts it, we will

> Sing with rapture and surprise,
> His lovingkindness in the skies.

I urge you to think over the truth of which I have been writing, that all God's lovingkindness to His people is marvelous.

How to See His Lovingkindness

My second remark is that we should desire to see this marvelous lovingkindness. The psalmist said, *"Show thy marvellous lovingkindness."* Likewise, we ought to ask God to let us see it; and that, I think, can be done in four ways.

With Our Minds

First, let each of us pray that we may see it with our intellects, so that we may adore Him. "Help me, O blessed Spirit, to see and understand what is the lovingkindness of God to my soul! I know that it is written of some that *'they shall understand the lovingkindness of the LORD'* (Ps. 107:43). Let me be among the number of those truly wise ones. O Lord, make me wise to see the end and design of Your providence as well as the providence itself! Make me wise to perceive how You have prepared Your grace to meet my depravity, how You adapt Your upholdings to the slipperiness of the way and to the feebleness of my feet. Often shed a ray of light upon some passage in my life that, otherwise, I could not comprehend; and let the light stay there until I begin to see and to know why You did this and why You did that. *'Show thy marvellous lovingkindness.'*"

I am sure, dear friends, that the lessons of a man's own life are too often neglected. But, in the life of any ordinary child of God—John, Mary, Thomas, or whatever the name might be—there is enough to fill anyone with wonder and admiration for the lovingkindness of the Lord, if his mind is sufficiently illuminated to see the hand of God in it and to see what God intended by it. He sometimes uses strange means for producing blessed results. With His sharp ax, He will cut down all our choice trees. As if by a whirlwind or a tornado, He will devastate our gardens and make our fields a desolation. He will do it all in order that He may drive us away from the City of Destruction and make us go on pilgrimage to the Celestial City, where the ax can never come and the leaves will never fade.

In His mysterious dealings with us, the Lord often seems to push us backward so that we may go forward and to flood us with sorrow so that He may immerse us in blessing. That is His way of working wondrously. If we could understand it, according to the prayer of the text, *"Show thy marvellous lovingkindness,"* we would be full of adoring wonder.

With Our Hearts

The next meaning I would give to this prayer would be, "Lord, show Your marvelous lovingkindness to my heart, that I may give You thanks. Lord, I know that You have been very good to me; but I pray You to show my heart how good You have been by letting me see how unworthy I have been of this Your kindness."

Sometimes it is very profitable to sit down and think about the lovingkindness of God, mingling with it humble reflections on your own shortcomings. If you do this, you will at last break out with a cry such as this: "Why is all this mercy shown to me?"

I know a dear brother in Christ, a clergyman, whose name is Curme; he divides it into two syllables, "Cur-me," so as to make it mean, "Why me? Why is all this goodness given to me, Lord?" And that is a question that I, too, would easily ask: "Why me, Lord?"

> Why was I made to hear thy voice,
> And enter while there's room;
> When thousands make a wretched choice,
> And rather starve than come?

Is this kindness, and that, and this, all meant for me? Can it really be intended for me? Such reflections as these will make me realize more than ever how *"marvellous"* is God's lovingkindness to me and will fill my soul with adoring gratitude and thanksgiving.

With Our Faith

We also ought to pray the Lord to show His *"marvellous lovingkindness"* to our faith, so that we may again confide in Him. If He will cause the eye of our faith to see that He has this *"marvellous lovingkindness"* toward us, we will be all the more ready to rely upon Him in all the straits into which we may yet be brought. Do you believe it, my dear friend? Brother or sister in Christ, do you believe that God loves you? You know how sweet it is to be sure that your child loves you. Though he may well do so because of his many obligations to you, yet it is sweet for his warm cheek to touch yours and to hear him say, "Father, I love you." But, oh! It is far sweeter for God to say, "I love you."

Read the entire Song of Solomon, and do not be afraid to make use of the message of that sweet and matchless Canticle. Hear in it the voice of Jesus saying to you, *"Thou art all fair, my love; there is no spot in thee"* (Song 4:7). *"Thou hast ravished my heart, my sister, my spouse; thou hast ravished my heart with one of thine eyes, with one chain of thy neck"* (v. 9). Such words as these may be sensuous to those who are sensuous, but they are deeply spiritual to those who are spiritual. Oh, the bliss of having such words as those coming from the Christ of God to us! Why, sometimes, when our Lord thus speaks to us, we hardly know how to bear our excess of joy!

I could not ask for a better vacation than to have one hour alone with Jesus Christ, to be undisturbed by any earthly care, and just to think of nothing else but the love of God—the love of God to me. Oh, that it now were shed abroad, in all its fullness, in this poor heart of mine (Rom. 5:5)! O love divine, what is there that can ever match your inexpressible sweetness? Truly, it is *"marvellous lovingkindness."* Again I ask you, reader, Do you believe this? Are you sure you do? Pray God to show it to your faith distinctly and clearly, so that you will be absolutely sure of it and truly depend upon it whenever you need it.

Through Our Experiences

One other meaning of the text may be, "Show Your *'marvellous lovingkindness'* to me now in my experience, so that I may rest in You. Let me now, at this present moment, O my God, experience something of that lovingkindness in my soul, in whatever condition I may happen to be, so that I may be so flooded with the consciousness of it that I may do nothing else but sit in solemn silence before You and adore You, while beholding the blazing splendor of Your love!"

We should desire to see His lovingkindness in all four of these ways: with our minds, with our hearts, with our faith, and through our experiences. I cannot write any more about this part of my subject, but must leave you to fill in the gaps. This is not a topic upon which one should venture to write, if he wants to say all that should or could be said upon it.

How His Lovingkindness Is Displayed

My third and final remark is that there are several ways in which we can see this *"marvellous lovingkindness"* of God displayed to us in its marvelousness. Let me try to make them clear to you.

As Pardon for Sin

First, we ought to see His lovingkindness displayed to us in that we have been pardoned of great sin. I expect that there is at least one among my readers whose sin weighs very heavily on his conscience. Your sin is very great, dear friend. I cannot exaggerate it, because your own sense of its greatness far surpasses any descriptions I could give. You feel that, if God were to pardon you, it would be a marvelous thing. If He were, in one moment, to take all your guilt away and to cause you to be completely forgiven, it would be a marvelous thing. Yes, it would; it would.

God is constantly doing wonders. Therefore, glorify His name by believing that He can work this miracle of mercy for you. Pray this prayer: "Lord, show forth Your marvelous lovingkindness in me." Do not be afraid even to sing,

> Great God of wonders! all thy ways
> Are matchless, God-like, and divine;
> But the fair glories of thy grace
> More God-like and unrivall'd shine:
> Who is a pardoning God like thee?
> Or who has grace so rich and free?

"Believe on the Lord Jesus Christ, and thou shalt be saved" (Acts 16:31), and saved immediately. Trust Him now, and though it will be marvelous to you, I have shown you that all of God's lovingkindness is marvelous and that the extraordinary is ordinary with God. The marvelous is but an everyday thing with Him. Pray for this *"marvellous lovingkindness"* to be manifested to you, and you will have it.

Someone once said, "If God ever saves me, He shall never hear the last of it." You may say the same. You may firmly resolve that, from this point forward, having had much forgiven, you will love much; having been saved from great sin, you will tell it on earth and tell it in heaven. And, if you could, you would even make hell itself resound with the wondrous story:

> Tell it unto sinners tell,
> I am, I am out of hell.

You would shout, "What is more, I am on the road to heaven, for God's *'marvellous lovingkindness'* has been shown to me."

As Deliverance from Trouble

So, God's lovingkindness may be seen as pardoning great sin. Next, we ought to see it as delivering us from deep trouble. I may be addressing some poor child of God who is sorely perplexed. These are very trying times, and I constantly encounter godly people who have a sincere desire to *"provide things honest in the sight of all men"* (Rom. 12:17), but who do not find it easy to do so. Some very gracious people have gotten into a bind, and they cannot imagine how they will get out. If this is your case, dear friend, I expect you feel very much as John Fawcett's hymn puts it:

> My soul, with various tempests toss'd,
> Her hopes o'erturn'd, her projects cross'd,

Sees every day new straits attend,
And wonders where the scene will end.

Well, now, if you are ever brought through all your troubles, it will be *"marvellous lovingkindness"* to you, will it not? Then, go to God with the prayer, *"Show thy marvellous lovingkindness,"* and He will do it. He will bring you up and out and through—perhaps not in the way you would like to come, but He will bring you out in the best way.

> *Trust in the LORD, and do good; so shalt thou dwell in the land, and verily thou shalt be fed. Delight thyself also in the LORD; and he shall give thee the desires of thine heart. Commit thy way unto the LORD; trust also in him; and he shall bring it to pass.* (Ps. 37:3–5)

Always expect the unexpected when you are dealing with God. Look to see, in God and from God, what you have never seen before. When you are dealing with Him, whose arm is omnipotent and whose heart is faithful and true, the very things that will seem to unbelief to be utterly impossible will be those that are most likely to happen. God grant you grace, dear friend, to use the prayer of our text as the means of delivering you from deep trouble!

As a Source of Joy

Besides seeing His lovingkindness as a source of pardon and deliverance, we ought to see it as a source of joy. I think we may do so by using our text as a prayer in this manner: "Lord, reveal Your marvelous lovingkindness to me, so as to give me high joys and ecstasies of delight."

I sometimes envy those good people who never go up and never go down, always keeping at one level; theirs must be a very pleasant experience indeed. Still, whenever I ascend to the heavenlies, then I go up far beyond anything I can describe. Whenever I do ride upon the clouds, then I do not envy the people who keep along the smooth road. Oh, what deep depressions some of us have had! We have gone down to the very bottoms of the valleys, and the earth has seemed to surround us. But, after just one glimpse of God's everlasting love, we have been up there where the lightning flashes, resting and trusting among the tempests, near to God's right hand.

I think, or rather, I am sure, we may pray for this experience. Should not the preacher of the Word wish to know the fullness of divine love? Should not the teacher of the young want to learn all that he can concerning God's infinite love? Though this is the love that passes knowledge (Eph. 3:19), should not every Christian wish to know all that is knowable of this great love of God? Then let us pray, *"Show thy marvellous lovingkindness."* It was truly said, *"Thou canst not see* [God's] *face...and live"* (Exod. 33:20); but I have been inclined to say, "Then, let me see God's face, and die."

John Welsh said, when God was flooding his soul with a sense of His wondrous love, "Hold, Lord, hold! I am but an earthen vessel, and You will break me." If I had been there, and I could have stood no more, I would have said, "Do not hold, Lord! Break the poor earthen vessel, let it go all to pieces! Let Your love be revealed in me!" Oh, that I might even die of this pleasurable pain of knowing too much of God, too much of the ineffable delight of fellowship with Him! Let us be very venturesome, beloved, and pray, *"Show thy marvellous lovingkindness."*

As a Means of Our Usefulness

And, when we have done that, I think we may pray this prayer for ourselves, so that we may see His lovingkindness as a means of our own usefulness. You want to do good, dear brother, dear sister. Well, then, pray to God, "Show me Your marvelous lovingkindness, O Lord! Use even such a feeble creature as I am. Let heaven and earth and hell itself see that You can save souls by poor, ignorant men as well as by inspired apostles and learned doctors. Lord, in my chapel, show Your marvelous lovingkindness. Crowd it with people, and bring many of them to Christ. In my class, Lord, show Your marvelous lovingkindness. If there never were a Sunday school class in which all were saved, Lord, let it be done in mine. Make it a marvelous thing."

One dear brother was praying at a prayer meeting before a church service, and he kept on pleading that God would bless the pastor again as he had done before. I like that prayer; it is as if the man meant to say to the Lord, "Whatever You did in years gone by, do the same over again. If ever it were a marvelous thing to see how the people thronged to hear the Word, Lord, make it more marvelous still."

I remember when some people called the early success of the Metropolitan Tabernacle, the church that I pastor, "a nine days' wonder." Well, it has been a good long nine days since then; but, oh, I hope that we might have another nine days like it—just another nine such days! May God be pleased to send us as many conversions as we had at the first—yes, even ten times as many!

If ever there have been revivals in the church of God that have been really marvelous, brothers and sisters, let us take up the cry, "Lord, show Your marvelous lovingkindness again. Send us another Whitefield and another Wesley, if such will be the kind of men that will bless the world. Send us another Luther, another Calvin, another Zwingli, if such will be the men who will bless the world. Lord, send us another Augustine or another Jerome, if such will be the men by whom You will bless the world. But, in some way or other, Lord, show us Your marvelous lovingkindness."

"Oh!" some would say, "but we do not want any excitement. That is an awful thing, you know, anything like excitement." And perhaps they would add, "We have heard so much of what has been done in previous revivals. It has all ended in smoke, and, therefore, we really dread the repetition of such an experience." Well, then, brother, you go home and pray, "Lord, show me Your moderate lovingkindness." When you are on your knees tonight, pray, "Lord, save a half dozen souls here and there; for

We are a garden wall'd around,
Chosen and made peculiar ground;
A little spot inclosed by grace
Out of the world's wide wilderness.

"Lord, make us yet smaller, press us still tighter, to the glory of Your blessed name!"

I don't think any of you can pray that prayer. You can pray it, if you like; but for my part I intend to pray, *"Show thy marvellous lovingkindness."* I hope many of you will join me in it, and may God hear us!

Oh, for some new miracle of mercy to be brought about in the earth! Oh, for some great thing to be done, such as was done in days and years gone by! Will it come about, or not? It will depend on this promise: *"Open thy mouth wide, and I will fill it"* (Ps. 81:10). But if our mouths are not open, we cannot expect to get the blessing: *"According to your faith be it unto you"* (Matt. 9:29). The Lord grant that our faith may expect to see His *"marvellous lovingkindness"* displayed yet more and more! Amen and Amen.